POLICY STUDIES IN EMPLOYMENT AND WELFARE NUMBER 11

General Editors: Sar A. Levitan and Garth L. Mangum

Sex in the Marketplace: American Women at Work

Juanita Kreps

The Johns Hopkins Press, Baltimore and London

This research was prepared under a contract with the Office of Manpower Research, Manpower Administration, United States Department of Labor, under the authority of the Manpower Development and Training Act.

The National Manpower Policy Task Force is a private non-profit organization of academicians who have a special interest and expertise in the area of manpower. The Task Force is primarily concerned with furthering research on manpower problems and assessing related policy issues. It sponsors three types of publications:

1. Policy Statements in which the Task Force members are actively involved as co-authors.

2. Studies commissioned by the Task Force and reviewed by a committee prior to publication.

3. Studies prepared by members of the Task Force, but not necessarily reviewed by other members.

Publications under Nos. 2 and 3 above do not necessarily represent the views of the Task Force or its members except those whose names appear on the study.

The Johns Hopkins Press, Baltimore, Maryland 21218
The Johns Hopkins Press Ltd., London

ISBN 0-8018-1278-X (cloth)
ISBN 0-8018-1277-1 (paper)

Originally published, 1971
Second printing, 1972

Paperback edition, 1971

331.4
K92

Contents

Preface

What does woman want? Dear God! What does she want?
—Sigmund Freud

The war to end discrimination against women is a popular war. Each side can be righteously indignant: the one demanding equality and freedom from oppression; the other staunchly defending home and motherhood. But rhetoric cannot obscure the overwhelming importance of the issues to American women and to their husbands, male employers and colleagues. Nor will the issues be resolved by Constitutional amendment or additional legislation, important as these measures are. For the problems go to the heart of our society, its organization and its expectations of women and men.

Despite the central significance of the movement for equal rights, it is not always possible to have the question taken seriously. Something in the stereotype of the female (or perhaps in that of the male) makes equal treatment for women seem sometimes unimportant, if not harmful. Is not the male role that of the protector, the female the protected? And if the protected gains equal status, would she not lose more than she gains? Even if women are to gain equality, it must come as a gift from men. A prominent educator, Rosemary Park, writes that in a discussion of minority student problems, she raised the question of whether women, too, should not be considered. The answer was: "You know we love the girls. We'll take care of them."

Of the many complex issues involved in the current controversy, the most glaring complaints have to do with the employment of women. Although their numbers in the labor force have increased dramatically in the past two decades, there is little drama in most of the jobs women enter. They continue to staff the clerical jobs, the elementary classrooms, and the sales rooms; they are almost never vice-presidents or high school principals or hospital administrators. Women argue that their pay is much lower than that of men; that the labor market is frequently divided into men's jobs and women's jobs; that there are significant wage differentials even when both are employed on the same job. In contrast to the situation of other minority or marginal groups who suffer an educational disadvantage, women claim that they are overeducated for most of the jobs they do.

Attempts to explain these phenomena of the job market have been few but substantive. A review of the analyses of the labor market behavior of women (particularly married women) reveals careful study of the significant supply variables; similarly, the sources of demand for women workers have been identified. One of the things that stands out is the impact of work discontinuity on a woman's career. Knowing that her first stint in the labor force will be a short one and that her reentry is unpredictable, depending on her husband's job, the availability of household help, and how many children she has, she is unlikely to think of a lifetime career when she is young. On her return to work, she finds few educational opportunities open to her. The split career thus effectively dampens interest in job preparation in youth when it could be acquired, and makes it more essential in middle age when educational resources are limited. It is curious that public interest in manpower training has shown so little attention to this need.

Studies of women in the labor force—their occupational status, demographic characteristics, earnings—leave many pieces of the puzzle missing. Most of the "why" questions remain unanswered. Why do women go into the same occupations, year after year? It is not difficult to explain, in simple demand and supply terms, why the wages in these over-supplied fields remain low; but why is a service offered when the wage is so low? And what effect can legislation have, if women do not switch to more rewarding jobs? Why has women's proportion of advanced academic degrees remained so low? Why, if it is partly the monotony of housework that drives a woman into the market place, is she willing to perform equally routine tasks in an office, without even the freedom to schedule the monotony in her own way? Is the difference merely the pay check? And does the fact that she is a secondary worker, whose pay is added to her husband's, mean that the pay can be quite low and still attract her into the market?

We know very little about intra-family decision making; in particular, we know little about the value a family places on the non-market services of the wife. What we do know should be disquieting to defenders of the notion that woman's place is in the home: a woman's wage in most market jobs is quite low and by implication so, too, is her value in the home. But for more than half the women who do not have market jobs, we can conclude only that their value in the home is higher than the market wage; and this conclusion holds only if market jobs are available. It is, in short, very difficult to discuss the value of women's work in and out of the market place when only the market job carries a price tag. And the notion of attaching a dollar value to homework may not be as silly as it first sounds.

The chapters which follow are intended to serve as a brief review of the literature on the subject of women's labor force activity, and to examine when women work, at what jobs, and under what arrangements. It will be necessary to raise questions throughout the review, however, since the ultimate purpose of any such survey is to identify the gaps in information. As will be readily evident, many aspects of women's work, both market and nonmarket, remain relatively unexplored. At a time when widespread attention is being focused on the rights of women, it seems particularly important to reexamine their work roles as well; to ask what conflicts the changing patterns of women's work may be generating. For while the current interest in women's equality is not limited to the area of jobs and careers, changes in labor force status are a critical part of the new movement. Until adequate information is available on the worklives of women, questions relating to equality of the sexes will be very difficult to resolve.

J. K.

Durham, N.C.

1
Introduction: Some Things We Know about Women

> Any part of mankind that has had to accept its self-definition from a more dominant group is apt to define itself by what it is *not* supposed to be. Thus, it is easy to impress on working women of some classes and pursuits the proposition that they should not be unfeminine, or unmaternal, or unladylike, all of which may well come in conflict with that identity element in many successfully intellectual women whose background decreed that, above all, they should not be unintelligent.
> —Erik H. Erikson

For many American women, the past few months have marked the summer of discontent. The rumblings began much earlier, however, in part a corollary of the overall thrust for equality and in part a symptom of the related rise in expectations. Women have explained the basis of this unrest in a series of scholarly, thoughtful essays which are of more interest, perhaps, to men than to other women who are inclined to feel that they understand the issues all too well.

In large measure, the discontent has to do with women's work: the problem of managing both a home and an outside job; the inferior status of women in the occupational hierarchy, particularly the absence of women in top business and professional jobs; sex differences in pay. In its first year of activity, the Equal Employ-

X ment Opportunity Commission, which received charges of discriminatory practices in alleged violation of Title VII of the Civil
Rights Act, found that almost 2,500 of the complaints (more than
a third of the total) were based on sex.

DIFFERENCES IN EARNINGS

The literature contains many references to the fact that women
earn less than men. Although sex differences in earnings will be
detailed in Chapters 2 and 3, some illustrative figures can be cited
in this introductory statement. Male year-round, full-time workers
had median earnings of $7,664 in 1968; the median for women
who worked full-time for the whole year was $4,457, or 58 per
cent of the male's rate. By occupational group, the differences are
also impressive (see Table 1.1). Even in the case of clerical work-

Table 1.1.   Median earnings of full-time year-round workers, by sex and occupational group, 1968

Major occupation group	Median wage or salary income		Women's median wage or salary income as percent of men's
	Women	Men	
Professional and technical workers	$6,691	$10,151	65.9
Nonfarm managers, officials, and proprietors	5,635	10,340	54.5
Clerical workers	4,789	7,351	65.1
Sales workers	3,461	8,549	40.5
Operatives	3,991	6,738	59.2
Service workers (except private household)	3,332	6,058	55.0

SOURCE: U.S. Department of Commerce, Bureau of the Census: *Current Population Reports*, P-60, No. 66.

ers, a group dominated by women, the median earnings of females
is less than two-thirds that of males. The explanation frequently
given for the male's higher wage is his greater experience on the
job. Yet a study revealed that 206 companies expected to offer

substantially different starting salaries to 1,970 men and women college graduates with the same undergraduate majors (Table 1.2).

Table 1.2. Expected salaries for June 1970 college graduates, by sex and selected field

	Average monthly salary	
Field	Women	Men
Accounting	$746	$832
Chemistry	765	806
Economics, finance	700	718
Engineering	844	872
Liberal arts	631	688
Mathematics, statistics	746	773

SOURCE: Frank S. Endicott, "Trends in Employment of College and University Graduates in Business and Industry." U.S. Department of Labor, Women's Bureau, February, 1970.

One of the factors holding down women's wages is their tendency to concentrate in low-paying jobs. One-fourth of all employed women now work in five occupations: secretary-stenographer, household worker, bookkeeper, elementary school teacher, or waitress. Entry into "men's jobs" is difficult, and access to the top levels of the better business and professional careers is often blocked by failure to consider women in making promotions to these jobs. Having been socialized to expect a certain niche in the occupational hierarchy, women continue to look for jobs where they know they can find them, and not to look toward areas traditionally closed to them.

Attempts to interpret the earnings gap have not been satisfactory, since there are so many variables involved. One author summarized the problem recently by noting that

analysts try to control for the difference in length of work activity during the year by comparing the earnings of women and men who worked the entire year at full-time jobs, but it is also necessary to allow for the fact that married women have restricted freedom of occupational choice. They may have to put convenience of location or flexibility of hours above earnings. Married women may not be in a

3

position to accept jobs with overtime pay or to accept a promotion to a job with heavier responsibilities. This may lead a wife to take a job which may not require her primary skill, or one in which she may not command the best salary.[1]

WORK, MARITAL STATUS, AND CHILDREN

Although women's wages and salaries have not caught up with those of men, there have been increases in the percentages of women who work, and some changes in the characteristics of the women who work outside the home. In 1970, about 31 million women were in the labor force, constituting 42 percent of all women age 16 and over; half a century ago the number was about 8 million, the proportion 23 percent.[2] In 1970, married women made up 60 percent of the female labor force, instead of 30 percent, as in 1940. To the young single woman of the earlier era work was a prelude to marriage and children, and once she left the working world she seldom returned. To the forty-year old married woman of today, who is in the second phase of her worklife, there is no need to withdraw until retirement—another 20 to 25 years. This growth in the numbers and proportions of women who work is all the more remarkable in view of the relatively low earnings cited above.

The worklife pattern of women has in the past involved a brief stint in the labor force during the late teens and early twenties, a period for childbearing and early child care, then a resumption of work from the mid-thirties to about age sixty. As Stuart Garfinkle has shown, worklife expectancy of women aged twenty who do not marry is about forty-five years; for wives who have no children it is thirty-five years. But even for wives with children the worklife is quite long—on the average, twenty-five years for the twenty

---

[1] Elizabeth Waldman, "Changes in the Labor Force Activity of Women," *Monthly Labor Review* vol. 93 (June, 1970), p. 15.

[2] Most of the statistics cited in this section are taken from *ibid.*, and subsequent articles in *Monthly Labor Review*, vol. 93 (June, 1970), by Janice N. Hedges, Robert D. Moran, H. M. Willacy and H. J. Hilaski, and Edmund Nash, pp. 10–44.

year old wife who has one child, twenty-two years when there are two children, twenty years with three, and seventeen with four or more children.[3]

The influx of older married women into the labor force is a fairly recent phenomenon. In 1940, the highest participation rates were for teenagers and women in their early twenties; after the teens and early twenties, the proportion of women who worked fell steadily. By 1950 older women were beginning to stay on the job or return to work, and by 1960 the proportion of older women who worked was as high as that of the young. The rate for older women continued to rise during the past decade, and that of young women rose even faster.[4] Although the dip during the twenties-to-early thirties is still evident, the magnitude of the drop is reduced (Figure 1.1). It seems likely that women's current interest in careers will have the effect of smoothing the curve even more during the 1970's.

The presence of young children reduces the probability of a mother's working, although mothers are more likely to continue working now than in the recent past. The participation rate for all wives is now about 40 percent. Among wives with no children under eighteen, the rate for wives under thirty-five years of age is 67 percent; for women over this age, 36 percent. Work rates of younger mothers are higher even when children are present—51 percent of young mothers with children six to eighteen years of age (compared with 48 percent for older mothers); 29 percent for mothers with children under six (and 27 percent for older mothers).[5] In total, 11.6 million mothers were working or seeking work in March of 1969, and one-third of these mothers had children under six years. About 9.7 million working mothers were in homes with husbands present; the other 1.9 million were widowed, divorced, or separated. Almost half the children under six years of age were cared for in their own homes, and almost a third more

[3] Stuart H. Garfinkle, "Worklife Expectancy and Training Needs of Women," U.S. Department of Labor, Manpower Report No. 12, May 1967.
[4] Waldman, "Changes", p. 11.
[5] *Ibid.*, p. 12.

Figure I.I LABOR FORCE PARTICIPATION RATES
OF WOMEN BY AGE, 1940 – 70

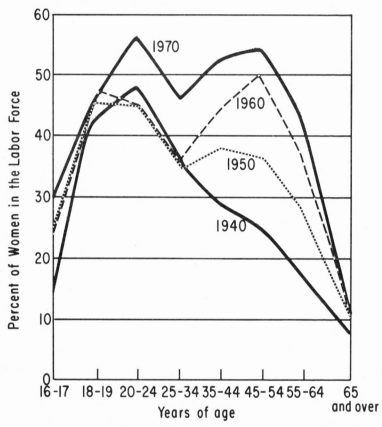

Source: <u>Monthly Labor Review</u> 93 (June, 1970), p. II.

in other people's homes. Only 6 percent had group care in child care centers or other group arrangements.[6]

SOME SPECIAL NEEDS:
NEGRO WOMEN AND WOMEN HEADS OF FAMILIES

Analysis of women's aggregate labor force activity obscures the necessarily high rates of participation by particular groups of women who have little option as to whether or not they will seek paying jobs. Women who are heads of households with children have income needs that are at least as pressing as those of men workers, except in cases where alimony and child support are available; in many instances the woman head-of-household has much greater need, since she must pay for child care while she works. And, while it is true that practically all girls will marry, divorces, separations, and deaths of husbands nevertheless leave an increasing proportion of families with female heads. In the past decade the number of families headed by women increased by 24 percent, whereas the number of all families grew by 14 percent.[7]

The need for income surely accounts in large part for the higher work rates of these women. In addition the low levels of income in many husband-wife families, particularly among nonwhites, makes it necessary for wives to seek jobs even when child-care responsibilities at home might well dictate a different preference. The relationship between income and family stability is complex, as Robert L. Stein has noted:

> When a breadwinner dies or leaves his family, the loss or reduction of financial support may be only partly offset by the wife's earnings and Social Security, private pensions or insurance, welfare payments or other benefits. Poverty or low income may itself create tensions leading to family breakup, or the fact that a man does not have a steady job at good pay may induce him to leave so that his family can obtain public assistance.[8]

[6] "Who are the Working Mothers?" U.S. Department of Labor, Women's Bureau, May, 1970.

[7] Robert L. Stein, "The Economic Status of Families Headed by Women," *Monthly Labor Review*, vol. 93 (December, 1970), pp. 3–10.

[8] *Ibid.*, p. 5.

The earnings and labor force status of Negro women

The proportion of Negro women in the labor force is higher than that for white females, although the magnitude of the difference has declined in recent decades. Negro wives had a 51 percent participation rate in 1969, as compared with the white wives' proportion of 39 percent. Negro wives are younger than white wives, but for any age, age of children or husbands, or incomes of husbands, the Negroes are more likely to work than are white wives. In the case of families having preschool children, 44 percent of the Negro and 27 percent of the white wives worked. In the case of families with husbands' incomes of $10,000 or more, half the Negro, but only one-third of the white, wives were in the labor force.[9]

It is nevertheless true that the prevalence of low family incomes is in large part the explanation for the higher labor force rates of non-white wives. In 1966, about one-third of all non-white families had incomes below the poverty level, as compared with less than one-tenth of the white families. Poverty families would, of course, be more numerous, except for the contributions which wives make to family income, pushing many of the white and non-white families over the poverty threshold. In the mid-sixties, 42 percent of all non-white husband-wife families would have been in poverty, but for wives' earnings; in these families, the contributions of wives meant that 19 percent of them lived in poverty.[10]

There is some evidence that the earnings of non-white women have been improving more rapidly than those of non-white men. In a study of the effect of changes in discriminatory practices on the relative earnings of non-white workers, Orley Ashenfelter concludes that while the earnings of non-white men were quite stable during 1950–66, those of non-white women have improved steadily. He attributes this increase to the movement of non-white women into the clerical occupations, where the well-paid white

[9] Waldman, "Changes", p. 12.
[10] U.S. Department of Labor, *Negro Women in the Population and in the Labor Force*, 1968.

women are employed. Such an occupational shift would have had little effect on the relative position of non-white men, however.[11]

The educational attainment of Negro women is slightly higher than that of Negro men; in 1966 the women were found to have a median of 10.1 years of schooling, as compared with 9.4 for the men. By comparison, the median for white women that year was 12.2 and for white men, 12.0. Among Negroes, 40 percent of the females and 47 percent of the males had less than 8 years of school; for college completion, the rates are practically the same: 3.2 for women and 3.3 for men. School enrollment figures are now better for Negroes than in the past, the males making larger gains than females. This is particularly true at the high school level; at ages eighteen to nineteen, 46 percent of the males but only 30 percent of the females remain in school.[12]

Negro families suffer disruptions more often than white families. Whereas 68 percent of white women are married with husbands present, only 52 percent of Negro women have this marital status. More than one-third of the Negroes are widowed, divorced, or separated, in comparison with one-fifth of the white women. As a result, black families are much more often headed by women: one-fourth of all Negro (but one-tenth of all white) families have a female head. Finally, the average Negro family is larger than the white, the former having 4.4 members, and the latter, 3.6.

Some of the possible implications of these factors are indicated below in the discussion of female-headed families. The overriding fact of low earnings on the part of Negro wives is a major consideration in any comparison. Among year-round, full-time workers, the median wage of the nonwhite woman remains far below that of other workers: a median of 71 percent of that of the white full-time female worker, 66 percent of that of the nonwhite male median, and only 42 percent of that of the white male in 1965. In March, 1969, 46 percent of all employed Negro women were private household workers or service workers outside the home (as

[11] Orley Ashenfelter, "Changes in Labor Market Discrimination Over Time," *The Journal of Human Resources*, vol. 5 (Fall, 1970), pp. 403–30.
[12] U.S. Department of Labor, *Negro Women*, table 4.

INTRODUCTION

compared with 19.2 percent of white employed women). Minimum wage coverage of private household workers is practically non-existent.

Women Heads of Families

A recent article by Stein, cited above, summarizes the work and income status of women who head families. Of the 5.6 million such families, 3.4 million had children—a family average of 2.4 children under 18 years of age. Most of the other 2.2 million families were headed by women over 45, whose economic lot was not as severe; families headed by women aged 45–64, without children, had a median income of $7,000, whereas younger (i.e., aged 24–44) women's families with children had a median of only $4,000.

Although women heads of families are disproportionately the less well educated, the low-income, and the minority-group women (one-third have an elementary education or less, while one-fourth of all women are similarly educated), a significant percentage have college degrees and some have substantial incomes. In general, the proportion of families with women heads declines as family income increases—from 63 percent of all families with incomes of $2,000 or less, to 2 percent of those with $10,000 and over. Among the poverty groups, families headed by women constitute a growing proportion; 47 percent of all poor families had a female head in 1969, as compared with 28 percent a decade earlier.

The labor force activity of women who head families is higher than that of women who are married, with husbands present. Forty-seven percent of the divorced, separated, or widowed women with children under six years of age worked in 1969; only 29 percent of the married women with young children worked. But women with young children find it difficult to work full-time or year-round. Although 70 percent of women family heads aged sixteen to forty-four worked during 1967, only 38 percent worked full-time throughout the year. Their incomes reflected the extent of their work: about half the families in which the woman head

10

worked part-time or part of the year were poor, in contrast to 16 percent of the families whose female head was fully employed. Among families in which the woman head did not work, three-fourths were in poverty.[13]

Interest in welfare reform—in particular, debate surrounding the Family Assistance Plan and its provision that welfare recipients take jobs or job training—has focused renewed attention on the employability of women with dependent children, and on the advisability of employing these women to work outside their homes even when work is available. One recent study, addressing the question of AFDC women's employability, analyzed two criteria: their employment potential (educational level and employment history) and employment barriers (poor health, lack of day care facilities, lack of jobs for which they are qualified, psychological problems). For 1968, 44.5 percent of the AFDC mothers had high employment potential; they had worked at some time at skilled blue-collar or white-collar jobs, or had completed twelve years of school, or both. This was a significant improvement over the 1961 percent of 25.3. Barriers to employment remained much the same during the decade, however. About a third of both the low- and the high-potential mothers had two or fewer barriers, and a similar proportion had three, four or more. High-potential women, although facing slightly heavier barriers than those with low job potential, nevertheless dropped off the assistance rolls much more quickly.[14]

Work preferences of different female groups

It is evident that the work choice is not a real one for most women who head families, nor for women in very low-income families, black or white. And while a very high proportion of these women may seek work (and when successful, provide all or a substantial portion of the family income), they are among the

---

[13] Stein, "Economic Status."

[14] Perry Levinson, "How Employable are AFDC Women?" *Welfare in Review*, vol. 8 (August, 1970), pp. 12–16.

least employable of all labor force participants. To what degree can training programs, child care centers, and higher levels of employment in general provide such women job opportunities? In cases where there are young children in the home, are employment inducements appropriate? Should income maintenance programs provide such supplements to income as are necessary for these families?

There is little similarity between the situation confronting women in these families and that facing the educated married woman whose husband earns a substantial income. Motivation to work, career aspirations, kinds of jobs available, presence of discrimination on the part of employers, and family pressures exerted by the woman's employment—these, and other factors are markedly different for the two groups. Therefore, when a general relationship exists between labor force participation and some other variable (husband's income, for example), it is well to remember that the aggregate data may conceal very important variations within the adult female population. It would be easy to exaggerate the extent of married women's preferences for market work *per se* or, to put it differently, to underestimate the desires of low-income women for freedom to work only within the home. It would be particularly misleading to draw any firm conclusion as to the love women (or men) have for certain types of jobs—domestic service, unskilled operative jobs, low-skilled, clerical, and sales work.

There has been surprisingly little research on the work activity and motivation of these women, perhaps because the need for income is such an obvious explanation.[15] One study devoted to women workers in southern rural areas asked the question, "What things about your . . . job do you like or dislike most?" Almost one-fourth of the women were domestics, another fifth operatives, and another fifth farm laborers or foremen. Favorable attitudes toward their work were directly related to level of earnings, even

[15] See, for example, *"Why Women Work,"* U.S. Department of Labor, Women's Bureau, 1968.

though the highest median earnings in any occupational group were extremely low. Attitude varied also by occupational classification, but not in the predicted pattern: managers, professional and technical workers commented favorably on their work, agricultural workers unfavorably, with domestics aligned with the first rather than the second group. Despite their low job level and earnings, most of the women liked their jobs; however, the authors concluded that the women's aspirations for improved levels of living was the primary motivation for work.[16]

Data are now beginning to appear from Herbert S. Parnes' surveys of labor force behavior and work attitudes. The five-year study includes a sample of women aged thirty to forty-four and one of women fourteen to twenty-four years old, with questions on current employment, work history, education and training, migration, earnings, income, family status, and health, as well as attitudes toward work. Information will also be available on the costs of child care and transportation for older employed women.[17]

WOMEN'S WORK ROLES: THE QUESTIONS

Women's participation in the labor force was the subject of several important studies during the past decade. Jacob Mincer and Glen Cain,[18] in particular, have analyzed the market-nonmarket

[16] Geraldine B. Terry and Alvin L. Bertrand, *The Labor Force Characteristics of Women in Low-Income Rural Areas of the South*, Southern Cooperative Series Bulletin No. 116 (June, 1966).

[17] Data tapes are now being prepared and may be obtained from the Chief of the Demographic Surveys Division, Bureau of the Census. Printed reports, when available, may be ordered from the Superintendent of Documents.

[18] Jacob Mincer, "Labor Force Participation of Married Women," in National Bureau of Economic Research, *Aspects in Labor Economics*, (Princeton: Princeton University Press, 1962), pp. 63–97; and Glen Cain, *Married Women in the Labor Force* (Chicago: University of Chicago Press, 1966). In addition, see Marvin Koster's unpublished doctoral dissertation, "Income and Substitution Parameters in a Family Labor Supply Model" (Uni-

13

work decisions of wives as they are affected by husbands' incomes, unemployment, presence of children, and race. As Cain points out, wives' work activity influences the turn of other major affairs.

Married women have become so important a segment of the labor force that attention to their patterns is necessary for a full understanding of many important economic problems: economic growth and the cyclical behavior of national income, the personal distribution of income, the effects of income taxes on labor supply, and birth rates.[19]

Interest in the rise in female labor force activity reflects in part a concern about the characteristics of the new woman worker—in particular her marital status, whether she has children, how old she is. The working pattern set by generations of young women during the first half of the century posed little threat to marriage and family formation,[20] or to intrafamily care of small children. But the increments to the supply of female labor are now coming increasingly from wives, from mothers, from older women. Some of the implications of this new look are of importance to the individual families of the women who are joining the work force. What new roles are emerging for the husbands? Who takes over the care of small children? Are the dependency relationships not drastically altered when the wife is a full-fledged contributor to

---

versity of Chicago, 1966); T. Aldrich Finegan, "Hours of Work in the United States: A Cross-Sectional Analysis," *Journal of Political Economy*, vol. 70 (1962); and the major study by William G. Bowen and T. Aldrich Finegan, *The Economics of Labor Force Participation* (Princeton: Princeton University Press, 1969), especially chapters 5–8.

[19] Cain, *Married Women* pp. 120–21.

[20] On the contrary, such work by women helped them to find husbands and this enabled them *not* to work for very long, according to a report on the working girl of 1888: "... Study ... might show that this rapid decrease of numbers employed after 25 years of age is due to the encouragement which employment gives to marriage. A woman who is willing to work honestly and faithfully, even at low wages, that she may be able to support herself, has certainly a better chance of securing a home suited to her status in life than the one who prefers to be supported by her friends." *Working Women in Large Cities*, Fourth Annual Report of the U.S. Commissioner of Labor, 1888, p. 62; quoted in the *Monthly Labor Review*, vol. 93 (June, 1970), p. 33.

the family's support? Will the aspirations of the woman eventually raise her own professional goals to compete with those of her husband and children?

Other questions are of broader economic import. What are the short- and long-run changes in the size, sex composition, and industrial mix of the labor force? Will an increase in the proportions of married women who work now mean a reduced birthrate and hence fewer workers a generation from now? What investments are needed in the form of job training for women, day care centers for children, greater flexibility in working arrangements for both parents? Can the long-run reduction in the numbers of persons in domestic service continue, as the need for this service increases? What are the implications for spending and saving, under the impetus of two incomes per family?

Finally, there are questions of economic growth and improvements in welfare. The flow of women into the labor force has shifted their efforts from nonmarket to market activities. The former work carries no price tags, and thus was not counted in the calculation of the national product; the latter does. Has the effect been to overstate the growth in product? Or is the family somehow performing the household chores that the wife formerly did, so that her market productivity is a net addition to total output? And if there is such a net increase in product, what value do we impute to that portion of the family's leisure that is foregone when the wife takes a job? The value of her other unpaid activities —volunteer community work, for example—also needs to be kept in mind.

Some appraisal of women's worth in alternative uses would be possible if we attached money values to house work, child care, community service—activities on which more than half of the women now spend their time. But less tangible benefits—attention, supervision, companionship, informal education and training—would be very difficult to price. Since we clearly value these services and commitments, the question becomes one of whether these functions can be performed by the women, along with their market work, or whether they can be shared more evenly with men. Conceivably, we might conclude that such supportive functions were of less value than the market work women could alternatively do, although this conclusion appears unlikely in view of the frequently expressed concern over the coldness and depersonalization of modern life.

If any event, the tools of economic measurement are not available, nor is the question of the worth of women in alternative roles altogether an economic question. It would clarify our thinking somewhat, however, if we could be more explicit as to the values we attach to the nonmarket work women normally do. The tendency to view as unimportant those services for which we do not pay a wage or salary is deeply ingrained in our thinking, and it becomes easy to make a case for taking a job that does pay an income. Should society want to encourage wives and mothers to remain in the home, the case for nonmarket work would have to be treated more persuasively than it has been in recent years. Many women apparently interpret the value of their nonmarket services to society, and even to their families, to be quite low; otherwise, they could not justify working for their present wage rates.

16

2

The Demand for and Supply of Women Workers

We must realize that the working wife and mother is not a modern invention. On the contrary, the nonworking full-time wife and mother is a phenomenon that only modern affluency, that is, modern technology, has made possible.

—Bruno Bettleheim

The factors affecting the demand for women's services and the willingness of women to join the labor force are in many respects the same influences that direct the activities of male workers. Increases in aggregate demand for goods, leading to greater demand for labor, generally lead to improved job opportunities for women as well as men. On the supply side, within some wage range women, like men, offer more labor as the wage rises. Conversely, cutbacks bring unemployment to workers of both sexes, the rate for women usually being higher than that for men.

But there are also important differences in both the demand and the supply conditions for men and women—differences that spring from society's expectations of each of the sexes. Most men, for most of their lives, are in school or at work; not to be one place or the other calls for an explanation. Most women work, too, but not necessarily in the marketplace. It has been generally accepted that women are in charge of households, and only after this primary responsibility has been discharged are they expected to come into the labor force. So whereas we go to some pains to explain the *absence* from the labor force of any significant number of males, it is the *presence* of females that we feel must be analyzed. Those women who enter the labor force, particularly if they are married, continue to attract attention, market work for females being regarded as somewhat out of character as long as there is home work to do. In the explanations of the labor force participation of women, authors have looked into unusual circumstances: absence of a husband or children; an age at which family responsibilities are minimal; very low family incomes; very high educational levels.

THE SUPPLY FACTORS

The probability of a woman's working is influenced first and foremost by her marital status. More than half of all single women are in the labor force, in comparison with about 40 percent of women who are married and living with their husbands. But these overall percentages conceal much wider differences in work rates at particular ages, and age in turn reflects the presence of children, which is an important factor in women's decisions to work. Single women reach their peak labor force participation rate in their late twenties, when more than 85 percent of them are at work. Married women of the twenty-five-to-twenty-nine and the thirty-to-thirty-four age groups, by contrast, are less likely to be at work, these being the prime child-rearing years; about 37 percent of these women are in the labor force. The highest activity rates for married women are not reached until age forty-five to fifty-four, when children are in school or out of the home altogether. Then more than 48 percent of the married women are in the work force.

The dramatic changes in work rates are seen in those for married, rather than single women. The proportion of single women now in the labor force (51.2 percent) is only slightly higher than the 1940 rate (48.1 percent), and is approximately the same as the 1950 figure (50.5 percent). Although a change in survey coverage is reflected in the 1967 data (when women age 16 and over were counted, in contrast to the earlier count of women age 14 and over), a much greater change in the proportion of married women at work is nevertheless apparent. Data reflecting the same statistical bias reveals that the 1969 rate for married women has risen to almost two and one-half times the 1940 figure: to 39.6 percent, as compared with 16.7 percent.

Since a very large proportion of the increase in labor force size during recent decades is attributable to the number of married women who poured into factories and offices and service establishments, the question of why this growth has occurred—and whether it will continue—is central to overall projections of growth in the nation's output. Leaving aside for the moment the question of a possible overstatement in GNP that may result from the movement of women from nonmarket to market activities,[1] consider the relationship between wives' propensity to work and the major variables: wage, age, and education level.

Labor Force Activity and Income of Husband

It is generally supposed that men work mainly for pay.[2] Even with this simplifying assumption, however, economists took a long time to agree on the manner in which the rate of pay affected the

[1] See Ismail Abdel-Hamid Sirageldin, *Non-Market Components of National Income* (Ann Arbor: Institute for Social Research, 1969).

[2] In their argument, psychologists Haire *et al.* emphasized the role of pay in motivating work by all persons: "The drive for private money gains— the profit motive—provides the main ideological cleavage in the world today. Deep down, everyone assumes that we work mostly for money. The most evangelical Human Relationist insists that it is important, while protesting that other things are too (and are, perhaps, in his view nobler). It would be unnecessary to belabor the point if it were not for a tendency for money drives to slip out of focus in a miasma of other values and other practices. As it is, it must be repeated: pay is the most important single motivator used in our organized society." E. E. Ghiselli, M. Haire, and L. W. Porter, "Psychological Research on Pay: An Overview," *Industrial Relations*, vol. 3 (1963), pp. 3–4.

amount of labor offered: higher wage rates were said to call forth more hours of work, or fewer, unless the number of hours remained unchanged.[3] In the case of married women workers, the relationship between the wage rate and the quantity of labor has been further obscured by the factor of the husband's income.

The evidence indicates that at any point in time, the higher the husband's income, the less likely is the wife to work outside the home. Through time, however, husbands' incomes have risen and wives' labor force participation rates have also increased. The seeming conflict between the conclusions drawn from cross-sectional and those from time series data was explained by Jacob Mincer, who showed that while husbands' earnings have been rising, wives' earning potentials have been rising also. The positive correlation of wives' desire to work with their own potential earnings more than offsets the negative impact of their husband's higher incomes, with the result that increasing proportions of wives joined the labor force each year.[4] Clarence Long raised the question of why the participation of Negro women (whose wages also increased) has not grown along with those of white wives;[5] however, the participation rates for Negro wives have in fact increased, albeit more slowly than those of white married women.[6]

Glen Cain has noted the relationship between the labor force participation of married women and their husbands' incomes, when

[3] See Joseph J. Spengler's review of the argument in "Product-Adding versus Product-Replacing Innovations," *Kyklos*, vol. 10 (Fasc. 3, 1957), pp. 267–77, particularly for the citations to earlier works: Adam Smith, *An Inquiry into the Nature and Causes of the Wealth of Nations* (Modern Library ed., New York, 1937), pp. 81–86; J. B. Say, *Traité d'économie politique* (Paris, 1841), Book II, Ch. 7, sec. 4; T. R. Malthus, *An Essay on the Principles of Population* (London: Variorum edition, 1961), pp. 140–43, 526–29, 680–96, 720–21; A. C. Pigou, *A Study in Public Finance* (London, 1929), 83–84, and *The Economics of Stationary State*s (London, 1935), pp. 163–64.

[4] Jacob Mincer, "Labor Force Participation."

[5] Clarence Long, "Comment," in National Bureau of Economic Research, *Aspects of Labor Economics* (Princeton: Princeton University Press, 1962), pp. 98–105.

[6] Glen Cain, *Married Women.*

children of various ages were present and when there were no children. For the decade of the 1950's he points to the substantial increase in the work activity of women with pre-school children, at all levels of husbands' income. For all wives fourteen years old and over with husband present, the participation rate fell as husbands' income rose, according to the data for 1951 (the one exception being a lower rate for the $7,000–$9,999 income than for the $10,000 and above). The same pattern held for wives twenty to forty-four years old. In 1960, the participation rate for all wives rose with the husbands' incomes up to the income of $5,000; after that, wives' work declined. For wives aged twenty to forty-four, the rate fell throughout the rise in husbands' incomes. At all income levels of husbands, larger percentages of wives worked in 1960 than in 1951, but the biggest increase occurred among those wives whose husbands were in the $3,000 to $10,000 range, and particularly the $7,000 to $10,000 bracket (Table 2.1 and Fig. 2.1).[7]

Table 2.1. Labor force participation rates of married women by income of husband, 1950 and 1959

Income of husband in previous year	All wives, aged 14 years and older		Wives aged 20–44	
	April, 1951	March, 1960	April, 1951	March, 1960
Average for all wives	25%	30%	28%	32%
Under $2,000	29%	30%	36%	41%
$2,000 to $2,999	28	32	32	37
$3,000 to $4,999	25	36	26	37
$5,000 to $6,999	16	30	15	29
$7,000 to $9,999	7	25	5	21
$10,000 and over	12	16	11	15

SOURCE: Jacob Schiffman, "Martial and Family Characteristics of Workers," *Monthly Labor Review*, vol. 84 (April, 1961), p. 263.

[7] *Ibid.*, pp. 2–3.

Figure 2.I LABOR FORCE PARTICIPATION OF WIVES 1951,1960, 1969 BY INCOME OF HUSBAND

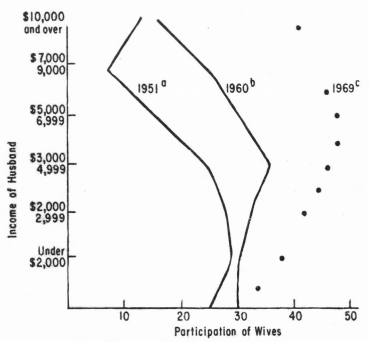

a = All wives, aged 14 and over
b = Wives aged 20-24
c = All wives, aged 14 and over

Source: Tables 2.I and 2.2.

As husbands' earnings continued to rise in the decade of the 1960's, wives' participation rates also rose. Table 2.2 shows higher

Table 2.2. Labor force participation of wives in March, 1969, by earnings of husbands in 1968

Earnings of husbands	Percent of all wives in labor force
$ 0–$ 999 (or less)	33
1,000– 1,999	38
2,000– 2,999	42
3,000– 3,999	44
4,000– 4,999	45
5,000– 5,999	47
6,000– 6,999	47
7,000– 7,999	45
8,000– 9,999	41
10,000– 14,999	35
15,000– 24,999	26
25,000 and over	18

SOURCE: Herman P. Miller, "Profile of The Blue-Collar American," in *Blue Collar Worker*, ed. Sar Levitan, (New York: McGraw-Hill, 1971, in press).

1969 labor force rates for wives with any given income of husband. The table indicates also that the higher the husbands' income the higher the wives' participation, up to the $5,000—$5,999 range, where the rate is 47 percent. Thereafter, the percentage of wives at work falls rapidly to a low of 18 percent for those with husbands' earning $25,000 or more.

From their 1964 data, James Morgan and his colleagues found a similar relationship between the percentage of wives who worked for money and the incomes of their husbands. Specifically, for all wives under sixty-five years of age, the variation was as follows: 37 percent of the wives whose incomes were $3,000 or less worked in 1964, while 55 percent of those with husbands' incomes of $3,000–$7,499, 42 percent of those with $7,500–$9,999, and 32 percent of those with $10,000 or more, were labor force participants.[8]

[8] James N. Morgan, Ismail A. Sirageldin and Nancy Baerwaldt, *Productive Americans* (Ann Arbor: University of Michigan, 1966), p. 48.

Labor Force Activity and Education

Wives' earnings are of course closely correlated with their educational achievement;[9] hence, the higher the level of education, the higher are wives' earnings and their rates of labor force activity. Morgan's figures for 1964 show the steady rise in the percentage of married women working, as their years of school completed rise.

Figures on work activity of all women reveal the same pattern. As Figure 2.2 indicates, college-educated women have higher participation rates than high school graduates, and high school graduates higher rates than women having completed elementary school, at all ages.[10] When age is disregarded, the work activity rate for all women (eighteen years of age and over) in 1968 showed the same rise with educational attainment, the range being from 17.4 percent for women with less than five years of school to 70.8 percent for those with five or more years of college (Figure 2.3).

Thus, highly educated women are likely to work for pay, whether or not they are married. The fact that these women earn higher salaries (see Figure 2.4), this advantage being reinforced by the greater appeal of jobs that are available to college-educated women, more than offsets the fact that in general these women are married to higher-income men, which would be expected to discourage the wives from working. The availability of ever-increasing numbers of educated women therefore makes it likely that the

[9] See U.S. Department of Labor, Women's Bureau, *Handbook on Women Workers*, Bulletin 294 (1969), pp. 140–41, for median earnings of women, by educational level, for 1966. For women twenty-five years of age and over, the medians at the major educational breaks were: eight years of elementary school, $1,404; high school, $2,673; college (four years) $4,165. In each of the first two categories, the median for white women is significantly higher than that for nonwhite; for college, the nonwhite median is higher: $3,964 as compared with $3,519 (Table 63).

[10] The exception to the upward progression of labor force activity with level of education occurs in the case of women with one to three years of college, who exhibit slightly lower work rates than high school graduates throughout most of their worklives.

24

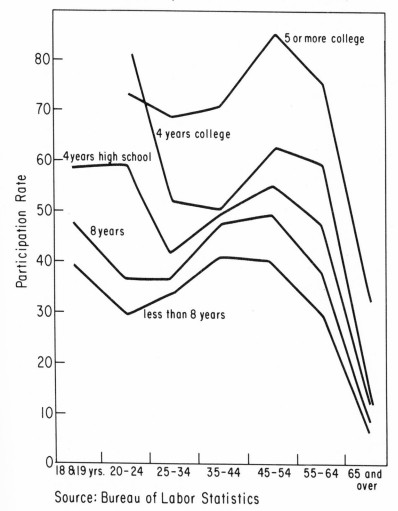

31

Figure 2.2 LABOR FORCE PARTICIPATION RATES OF WOMEN, BY YEARS OF SCHOOL COMPLETED AND AGE, 1968 (18 YEARS AND OVER)

Source: Bureau of Labor Statistics

25

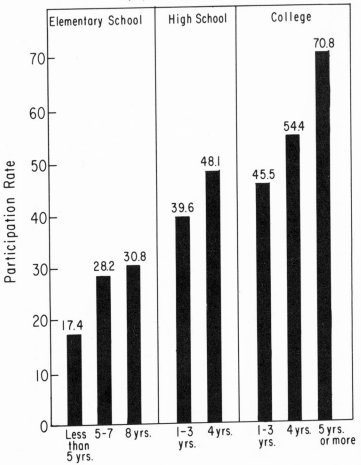

Figure 2.3. LABOR FORCE PARTICIPATION OF WOMEN, BY YEARS OF SCHOOL COMPLETED, 1968 (18 YEARS AND OLDER)

Source: Bureau of Labor Statistics

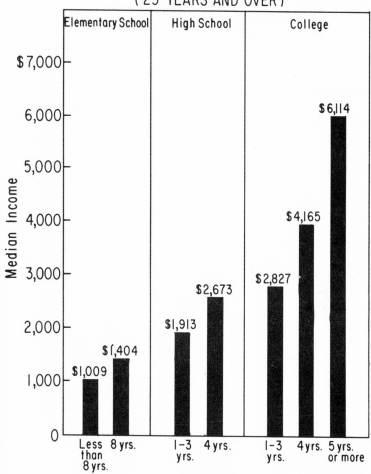

Figure 2.4. MEDIAN INCOME OF WOMEN, BY YEARS
OF SCHOOL COMPLETED, 1966
(25 YEARS AND OVER)

Source: Bureau of the Census

upward drift of female labor force activity will continue as long as the economy continues to demand workers of higher and higher educational achievement.

Labor Force Activity and Age

The pattern of women's labor force activity differs from that of men in several respects, the most obvious being the change associated with age. The proportion of men at work rises steadily with age up to about age thirty, and more than ninety percent remain in the labor force till the mid-fifties. Then the rate falls— at first gradually, then at age sixty-five quite abruptly. About one in four men over sixty-five currently remain in the work force. For women there are two rises in participation, and two declines. Their working proportion typically increases from entry till the early or mid-twenties, declines sharply for the next ten-year age group, and then starts to rise again in the mid-thirties. The second peak is reached at about age fifty, with the second decline reaching about ten percent for the women aged sixty-five and over (Figure 2.5).

For married women, the explanation for entry, withdrawal, and reentry to the labor force lies of course in their need to time their work activity to coincide with marriage, child-bearing and child-rearing. In particular, women with young children have been reluctant to work, unless the absence of a father made work necessary. In 1967 only 23 percent of the mothers with children under three (and fathers present) were in the labor force; 32 percent of mothers with children aged three to five worked. Among mothers of children aged six and over, 45 percent were on the job. In fatherless homes, the proportions who worked were much higher: 44 percent of the mothers with very young children, 59 percent with children three to five, and 75 percent of those with school-age children.

The coincidence of heavy family (particularly child-care) responsibilities with the ten-year span beginning in the early to mid-twenties has in the past accounted for the withdrawal of women in

Figure 2.5. LABOR FORCE PARTICIPATION RATES OF
MALES AND FEMALES, BY AGE, 1969

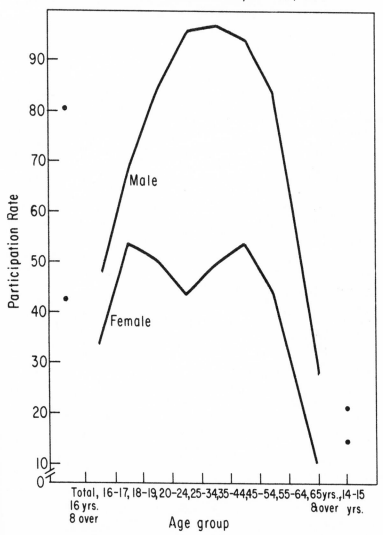

Source: Manpower Report of the President, 1970

this age bracket from the active labor force. But there is now substantial evidence that more women are beginning to stay on the job through the period of early child-rearing, and the "drop-out" rate for women in their twenties and early thirties may be lower in the future. Between 1964 and 1969, participation rates for twenty-to-twenty-four-year-old mothers of children under six rose from 24 to 33 percent, and for twenty-five-to-thirty-four-year-old mothers of children under six it rose from 22 to 27 percent. Women's current clamor for day-care centers would seem to indicate a desire to work during this period, if arrangements for children are available.

For women who never marry, or who are widowed, divorced, and separated, worklife is less often interrupted. Never-married women nevertheless reach their maximum rates of participation in their mid-twenties, after which there is a gradual decline until age sixty and a sharp drop thereafter. The proportion of widowed, divorced, and separated women who work rises steadily up to the age of about fifty, then declines in the same pattern. Any significant movement of women into these categories will tend to raise the female participation rate at all ages, but particularly in the twenties and early thirties when women in the "married, spouse present" classification are now most likely to desert the work force for domestic duty.

Summary: The Supply Factors

The major variables affecting the supply of working wives are thus: the income of the husband, the wife's level of education, and her age (which reflects the likelihood of the presence of children). James Morgan and his associates conclude, in fact, that "the effects of age, education, and husband's income are so powerful that they must be allowed for before one can search for the effects of other variables without the danger of making spurious correlations."[11] Specifically, the authors find that for the 1,640 wives in their 1964 study, these three variables "explained 13 percent of

[11] Morgan, Sirageldin, Baerwaldt, *Productive Americans*, p. 46.

the variance. The overall standard deviation of the proportion is 0.5. None of the (other) variables could explain as much as 0.5 percent of the total sum of squares by a single division of the whole sample."[12]

Other predictors of wives' labor force status had little overall effect: disability; illness or unemployment of the husband; size of town lived in; presence of preschool children; race. The effect of preschool children (which made a 7 percent difference in the proportion of wives who worked) was taken into account in the age of the wife. As for race, it was clear that Negro wives were more likely to work. But when age, education, and husband's income were held constant, the Negro-white difference in participation was quite small.[13]

Concluding that these three variables comprise the most important combinations of constraints on work and pressures to work, the authors then used a second-stage analysis for examining the effects of residuals. The husband's attitude toward mothers' working; whether the husband was self-employed (or working); whether there was a child in college; the number of people in the family; and several other variables including the first-stage factors of education and age of wife, and husband's income, were considered. The discriminants further affecting the wife's propensity to work were the husband's attitude (which made an 18 percent difference in the probability of the wife's working); his degree of achievement orientation, and his religious preference. The interaction of these second-stage variables with the primary ones was emphasized:

. . . When a wife has children at home and a husband who does not approve of mothers working, she is usually discouraged from working beyond what one would expect from her age and education and her

[12] *Ibid.*, p. 50.

[13] The participation of white women in husband-wife families is significantly lower than that for Negroes and other races, when other variables are not controlled. For whites, the highest rate among occupational groups was for clerical and sales workers, in which 49 percent of the wives were in the labor force in 1970. For Negroes and other races, the overall rate was 57 percent.

31

husband's income, already accounted for. The effect of the husband's disapproval is stronger if the husband is not highly achievement-oriented. The husband's *approval* also has more effect if his index of achievement orientation is low. . . .[14]

In summary, the participation rates and worklife pattern of single women, and those of women who are widowed, divorced, or separated, observe patterns that are quite different from those of married women (Figure 2.6). Changes in the rates in the past

Figure 2.6 LABOR FORCE PARTICIPATION RATES OF WOMEN BY AGE AND MARITAL STATUS, 1969

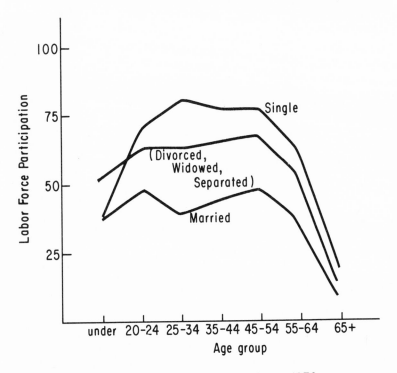

Source: Manpower Report of the President, 1970

[14] *Ibid.*, p. 58.

three decades have been much more pronounced for married women, particularly older married women. The key questions related to the growth in the supply of womanpower therefore have to do with the factors accounting for the increased labor force activity of married women. The most important variables—the woman's age and education, and her husband's income—seem to account for most of the variation in her willingness to work. What must now be examined in detail are the *demand* factors: what are the sources of demand for working women, and how much of the changing sex composition of the labor force is attributable to the force of demand?

THE DEMAND FACTORS

In directing attention to the factors influencing the supply of women workers, particularly the supply of married women workers, economists have of course taken the wage schedule into account. In fact, one of the major contributions to our understanding of a wife's work behavior was Mincer's work, cited above, which demonstrated the influence of both the husband's income, which has a negative (income) effect, and the wife's earnings which has a positive (substitution) effect. When we turn to an examination of the factors influencing the demand for women's work, however, we find fewer analytical studies,[15] although it is readily apparent that

[15] In an article published more than two decades ago, Hazel Kyrk emphasized "the pull and the push" influences on women's labor force participation:

"Favorable social attitudes, small families, decreasing and easier home production are not . . . to be thought of as the causes of gainful employment of women. The can opener or its more up-to-date equivalent, the frozen food package, is not a cause but a condition that facilitates. Women enter the labor market not because it is possible in the sense that they are not tied to their child care or by the disapproval of family or friends. They enter in response to the pull of attractive job opportunities or the push of economic necessity. It takes a greater pull or push to get them there if home conditions are not favorable, a lesser force if conditions facilitate; but the immediate cause is the attractiveness of the job opportunity or the need for the money the job will provide."

Hazel Kyrk, "Who Works and Why," *The Annals of The American Academy of Political and Social Science,* vol. 251 (May, 1947), p. 49.

the pace of growth in demand for different types of labor has differed markedly since the end of the Second World War.

It seems important to emphasize a rather obvious question: to what extent is the growth in the size of the female labor force attributable to the growing availability of jobs that women have traditionally done—or that employers would expect women to do? Such employer expectation would likely be reflected in the wages offered for these jobs. But there is something more involved. For in the case of women, perhaps as much as with the earlier view of Negroes and other minorities, there appear to be areas of work that are their special province. If these jobs are growing in numbers and in proportion to all jobs, then employers' expectations are likely to be such that they seek a larger female work force, not merely a larger work force.

The demand-pull effect on women's market work has been analyzed and documented in a recent Ph.D. dissertation. To illustrate the rapid growth in the demand for female labor, Valerie K. Oppenheimer shows the trend in numbers of women in "female" occupations (those in which 70 percent or more of the workers are female—nurses; stenographers, typists, and secretaries; private household workers; teachers; telephone operators; certain types of operatives, etc.) during this century. The percentage increases in recent decades were: 1940–50, 21.2 percent; 1950–60, 40.4 percent. The 40 percent rise in the demand for female labor during the nineteen-fifties meant not only that more jobs were available to women, but that the jobs were those which women were accustomed to doing—which society found acceptable for women to perform, and which women themselves expected to perform.[16]

For the 1950–60 decade, the author found that almost half of the net increase in the number of employed females occurred in

[16] Valerie K. Oppenheimer, *The Female Labor Force in the United States,* (Berkeley: Population Monograph Series, No. 5, University of California, 1970), chapters 3 and 5. For an earlier analysis of balkanization, see Clark Kerr, "The Balkanization of the Labor Market," in E. Wight Bakke *et al., Labor Mobility and Economic Opportunity* (New York: John Wiley and Sons, Inc., 1954).

occupations in which at least 70 percent of the workers were women, and almost 60 percent of the increase occurred in occupations which had a majority of women (Table 2.3). Since almost

Table 2.3. **Net growth from 1950 to 1960 in female employment attributable to growth in occupations dominated by females in 1960**

| | *Percent of total net growth due to net growth in occupations:* | |
	50 percent or more female in 1950	*70 percent or more female in 1950*
Total employed females	59.2	47.5
Professional, technical and kindred workers	65.8	54.4
Clerical and kindred workers	66.1	66.1
Operatives	66.6	29.3
Private household workers	100.0	100.0
Other service workers	93.7	44.2

SOURCE: Oppenheimer, *The Female Labor Force*, p. 160.

one-third of the women workers in 1960 were in residual jobs that could not be classified precisely, the 50-to-60 percent growth that was attributable to the swell in predominately "female" occupations is even more impressive. In conclusion, she notes that

There is substantial evidence that the demand for female labor has been increasing over the years. Furthermore, this rising demand can to a large extent be attributed to a rise in the demand for workers in typically female occupations—clerical work and several occupations in the professional and service categories. On the whole, this suggests that perhaps the best explanation for the overall increase in female labor force participation in recent years is that there has been an increase in the *demand* for female workers which has, in turn, stimulated an increase in the *supply* of women to the labor market.[17]

Evidence as to the segregation of male and female labor markets, presented by Oppenheimer as well as earlier writers, is quite persuasive. The balkanization of much of the labor market into female and male jobs is given implicit sanction in our thinking:

[17] *Ibid.*, p. 160.

the job classification "secretary," for example, denotes not just job skills, but female gender; nursing is so sex-typed that one must make explicit the exception by specifying "male nurse." Even when an overall function is performed by both sexes, as in the case of teaching, segments of the profession are dominated by one sex or the other: elementary school teachers are women, almost without exception, and college professors are more likely to be men.

The occupational composition of the female labor force itself has shifted somewhat since 1940. The major growth (as a percentage of all women employed) occurred in clerical workers, which then employed one out of five women and now employs one in three. Service workers (except private household) have increased by about one-fourth: from 11.3 to 15.6 percent of all employed women. Heavy declines reduced household workers' share of all women workers from 17.6 to 7.2 percent, and operatives from 18.4 to 14.8 percent. In terms of the percentage of all persons employed in the various occupational groups, women's share of professional and technical workers dropped significantly (from 45.4 to 38.6 percent of the total), and rose in other occupations: clerical workers (from 52.6 to 72.6 percent), service workers, except private household (40.1 to 57.0 percent), sales workers (from 27.9 to 39.7 percent), and also managers, officials and proprietors; for operatives and for private household workers, see Table 2.4.

In light of the thesis that male and female labor markets are balkanized, one might raise again the familiar question: has women's appearance in the labor force had the effect of displacing men from actual or potential jobs? The answer would seem to be no. Rather, the concentration of women in the accepted female occupations of elementary teaching, nursing, clerical and service-type jobs would seem instead to indicate some reluctance on the part of women to venture into men's occupational territory, or some reluctance on the part of employers to offer men and women wider job options, probably both.

Certain supply conditions have fostered the continuation of such segregated markets: the availability of low-priced female labor, both skilled and unskilled; women's reliance on the utilization of

36

Table 2.4.   Major occupation groups of employed women, 1940, 1950, 1968[1]

(women 14 years of age and over)

Major occupation group	Percent distribution			As percent of total employed		
	1968	1950	1940	1968	1950	1940
Total	100.0	100.0	100.0	36.6	29.3	25.9
Professional, technical workers	14.4	10.8	13.2	38.6	41.8	45.4
Managers, officials, proprietors (except farm)	4.3	5.5	3.8	15.7	14.8	11.7
Clerical workers	33.3	26.4	21.2	72.6	59.3	52.6
Sales workers	6.8	8.8	7.0	39.7	39.0	27.9
Craftsmen, foremen	1.1	1.1	.9	3.3	2.4	2.1
Operatives	14.8	18.7	18.4	29.9	26.9	25.7
Nonfarm laborers	.4	.4	.8	3.5	2.2	3.2
Private household workers	7.2	10.3	17.6	97.6	92.1	93.8
Service workers (except private household)	15.6	12.6	11.3	57.0	45.4	40.1
Farmers, farm managers	.3	1.5⎱	5.8[2]	4.1	5.5⎱	8.0[2]
Farm laborers, foremen	1.7	3.9⎰		28.0	27.4⎰	

[1] Data are for April of each year.
[2] Not reported separately in 1940.
SOURCE: *Handbook of Women Workers*, 1969, Table 40.

skills acquired in the course of performing their traditional roles; lack of pre-job training for women; their geographical immobility, and most of all, perhaps the attitudes of both sexes as to what constitutes appropriate male and female jobs.[18] The availability of cheap female labor, as Oppenheimer concedes, is a supply factor. But "if employers adapt themselves to such a labor supply so that the job in question acquires a 'female only' label, then the demand is not just for cheap labor, but for cheap *female* labor." Moreover, males are not likely to acquire whatever skills are required for female jobs; hence, employers cannot find men who can do women's jobs. Supposedly sex-linked characteristics of some jobs (physical strength, patience, manual dexterity) tend to make demand sex-specific, thereby promoting the continued labeling of these occupations.[19]

What of the future demand for women workers? Are the sex labels on jobs disappearing? And if so, will the widened career options for both sexes lead to an increase in the number of jobs offered to women, or to a decrease? One author recently warned that the professional job market for women was in trouble, in part because of increasing competition from men in such fields as teaching, library science, and health services. The competition will intensify, moreover, as the demand for some male-dominated occupations declines. When the male intrusions into formerly female-oriented professions are coupled with the growing numbers of women seeking jobs, women's job prospects do not appear promising.[20]

As in the case of all projections of labor requirements, the predictive difficulties lie with the problems of estimating the level of aggregate demand for goods and services. But accuracy in predicting the demand for labor of any particular type is susceptible also to errors in estimates of the *composition* of demand. Will there be heavy public expenditures for urban transportation, housing,

[18] *Ibid.*, chapter 3.
[19] *Ibid.*, p. 120.
[20] John B. Parrish, "Coming Crisis in Women's Higher Education and Work," *AAUW Journal*, vol. 64 (November, 1970), pp. 17–19.

and anti-pollution measures as opposed to education, for example? And if so, will women be as readily accepted in these newer areas as they have been in primary and secondary education and health-related professions?

A recent report from the Bureau of Labor Statistics points up the need for women to shift their occupational plans away from elementary and secondary teaching. Citing the current rate of growth in women graduates, the report predicts an over-supply of teachers by 1980, unless women are urged to consider social work, chemistry, engineering, and other areas indicated in Table 2.5.

Research on the demand for women workers has been scant, perhaps because economists have not thought of the labor market as being balkanized. Still, it would be instructive to have break-downs of estimated labor force requirements by sex, based on dif-

Table 2.5. Employment by occupation in 1968 for college graduates, and projected labor force requirements for 1980

Occupation	Estimated 1968 employment	Projected 1980 requirements	Percent change	Estimated supply
Chemists	130,000	200,000	55.7	Significantly
Counselors	71,000	107,000	49.8	below
Dietitians	30,000	42,000	40.3	requirements
Dentists	100,000	130,000	31.7	
Physicians	295,000	450,000	53.1	
Physicists	45,000	75,000	63.9	
Engineers	1,100,000	1,500,000	40.2	Slightly short of
Geologists and				requirements
geophysicists	30,000	36,000	20.6	
Optometrists	17,000	21,000	23.5	
Architects	34,000	50,000	47.1	In balance with
Lawyers	270,000	335,000	22.7	requirements
Pharmacists	121,000	130,000	7.0	Slightly above requirements
Mathematicians	70,000	110,000	60.5	Significantly
Life scientists	168,000	238,000	40.8	above
Teachers, elementary				requirements
and secondary	2,170,000	2,340,000	7.8	

SOURCE: Bureau of Labor Statistics, *College Educated Workers, 1968–80* (1970).

ferent assumptions as to the degree of overlap in certain occupations. The gross projections of future labor needs in jobs traditionally held by women, cited later, provide little detail and no analysis.

MALE-FEMALE DIFFERENCES IN EARNINGS

Balkanization of the labor force into male and female jobs helps to explain the significant differences in median earnings of men and women. Yet large differences persist, even when job classification, years of school completed, and other variables are held constant; in short, male earnings exceed those of females when there is occupational overlap, and both sexes are doing the same work.

Women's Earnings How Low are They?

As figures cited earlier indicate, the median incomes for the two sexes differ significantly. For year-round, full-time workers, the female median is 58 percent of the male's; $4,457 as compared with $7,664. The sex-related difference in earnings of full-time workers has been increasing, moreover; in 1956, the female median was 63 percent of the male's.

Insofar as the level of formal education warrants a bonus in pay, women again fall short of the mark. Many of the occupational groups in which women are heavily concentrated pay low wages while requiring higher-than-average educational achievement. Oppenheimer illustrates this phenomenon for several occupational groups in which women make up more than half the work force (Table 2.6). The median number of years of school completed by males and females in these occupations is higher than the median for the total male labor force: yet the median income (for males or females) in these female-dominated occupations does not compare favorably with the median for all male workers. She concludes that higher levels of education do not pay off for either men or women in these "female" occupations, which employ 71 percent of all women in professional and technical work, 98 per-

Table 2.6. Relative income and educational standing of selected occupations, 1960[a]

Occupation	Ratio of median number of school years completed in occupation to median for total male labor force[b]		Ratio of median income in occupation to median for total male labor force[c]	
	Male	Female	Male	Female
TOTAL	1.00	1.09	1.00	0.59
Professional Workers				
Dancers and dancing teachers	1.12	1.12	0.83	0.61
Dietitians and nutritionists	1.14	1.19	0.76	0.68
Librarians	1.50	1.46	1.01	0.77
Musicians and music teachers	1.34	1.33	1.03	0.29
Nurses	1.17	1.19	0.84	0.71
Recreation and group workers	1.36	1.32	1.00	0.78
Social and welfare workers	1.49	1.48	1.04	0.87
Religious workers	1.47	1.21	0.77	0.49
Elementary teachers	1.53	1.48	1.03	0.85
Teachers, n.e.c.	1.48	1.45	1.10	0.74
Therapists and healers	1.48	1.45	0.97	0.83
Clerical workers				
Library attendants & assistants	1.23	1.18	0.55	0.54
Physicians' and dentists' office attendants	1.12	1.12	0.68	0.53
Bank tellers	1.14	1.12	0.84	0.63
Bookkeepers	1.14	1.12	0.89	0.64
File clerks	1.12	1.10	0.75	0.59
Office-machine operators	1.13	1.12	0.96	0.68
Payroll & timekeeping clerks	1.13	1.12	1.00	0.73
Receptionists	1.13	1.13	0.77	0.57
Secretaries	1.15	1.14	1.05	0.71
Stenographers	1.14	1.14	1.02	0.70
Typists	1.13	1.13	0.80	0.64
Telephone operators	1.11	1.10	1.07	0.67
Cashiers	1.08	1.08	0.78	0.53
Clerical workers, n.e.c.	1.12	1.12	0.99	0.66
Sales workers				
Demonstrators	1.08	1.09	—[d]	0.50
Hucksters and peddlers	0.92	1.09	0.82	0.16

SOURCE: Valerie K. Oppenheimer, *The Female Labor Force*, pp. 100–101.

[a] Includes occupations in which at least 51 percent of the workers were female and where the median school years completed was greater than 11.1—the median for the total male experienced civilian labor force.

[b] Experienced civilian labor force.

[c] Wage and salary workers in the experienced civilian labor force who worked 50–52 weeks in 1959.

[d] Base not large enough to compute a median.

cent of all women in clerical jobs, and 42 percent of all female workers.[21]

Data cited earlier reveal differences in earnings by occupational group. In 1968, the annual median for full-time, year-round male professional and technical workers was $10,151; for females, it was $6,691. Figures for other occupations included $7,351 for male clerical workers, $4,789 for female; $6,738 for male operatives (mostly factory workers), $3,991 for women; $6,058 for male service workers, $3,332 for females; $8,549 for men salesworkers, $3,461 for female (Table 1.1).

Since length of service on the job surely affects wage and salary, and since most married women leave their jobs for a domestic tour of duty, it follows that some portion of the male-female difference in pay for a particular job classification could be attributed to the greater continuity of the male's worklife. For comparison, one needs wage and salary data for members of both sexes, by job classification, educational level, and length of time on the job. Thus, a comparison of the earnings of male and female high school graduates who have been retail sales clerks for five years, in similar types of establishments in a particular locality, would permit generalization. Although data of such detail are not generally available, researchers have drawn some tentative conclusions from the data on male and female earnings in the academic profession—one of the few areas in which several of the variables can be controlled. These findings are described in the next chapter.

Women's Aspirations: How High are They?

Further documentation of sex-related differences in earnings is perhaps not necessary; the data indicate that being male pays some wage premium within many of the occupations which utilize workers of both sexes. But a more important source of bias, perhaps, lies in the woman's selection of her occupation. If women persist in going into those jobs which have traditionally paid low

[21] *Ibid.*, pp. 99–101.

42

wages, improvements in pay scales can occur only if the demand for these services far outstrips the plentiful supply of workers. The reasons why women select these jobs invite further study. Are there nonmonetary rewards in certain careers that more than offset the low pay? Is elementary school teaching appealing to women because they like the work itself, or because it is viewed as an extension of their feminine roles, or because it can be timed to enable women to perform their regular household duties? How much are women willing to pay (in foregone earnings) for time free of market work at the time of day and year that nonmarket work is heaviest?

Clarence Long emphasized the importance of the short workday to a woman with a reference to her need to be able "to type till five o'clock, and still have time to shop for a cheap roast or a rich husband."[22] His quip raises an important question: Are the market-work–nonmarket-work–leisure choices for women not quite different from those of men? Mincer and Cain have stressed this difference in explaining the larger substitution effect in wives' labor supply; it is nonmarket work (not leisure) that is the substitute for their market work: "In the face of rising incomes and rising wages market work declines for males and single women and their leisure increases, while homework declines for wives and their leisure and their market work both increase."[23]

But it is not merely that their nonmarket work influences their decision as to whether to enter the labor force; the demands of home and family also influence *which* market jobs women are willing to take. Moreover, the period of heaviest domestic responsibility occurs fairly early in a woman's worklife, when she is likely to be forced to make some quite long-range decisions: whether to acquire further job training, or additional formal education; how many children she will have; whether to continue

[22] Clarence Long, *The Labor Force Under Changing Income and Employment* (Princeton: Princeton University Press, 1958).

[23] Cain, *Married Women*, p. 7. There may be some dispute (on the part of working wives) as to whether their leisure has increased as they have taken jobs outside the home.

working, at least part-time, during the child-bearing period. In the face of the demands on her time the young wife is likely to find that the scheduling of her job is the most important single consideration. Her immediate job choice is dictated in large measure by the time constraint imposed in the short run, and this choice in turn directs her subsequent career development.

Laments for wasted womanpower have now reached the popular press. Privately, women have mourned their underutilized and underpaid talents and education for decades. Although the implied understatement of the present worth of women's work in the non-market sphere calls for reexamination,[24] a recognition of the constraints on women's career choices is a first step in unravelling the complex problem of the low wages accorded to women's jobs, and the tendency for women to remain in those jobs.

Why do women not opt more often for occupations that are dominated by males, yet include some women in their ranks? The movement of both men and women into computer programming is a case in point, albeit an unusual one, since the job itself was new and lacking in traditional taboos. Yet most white-collar jobs are changing in content, giving some scope for integration of the sexes. Is it inevitable that in insurance companies men sell insurance and women do the typing? That in banks men make mortgage loans while women are tellers? Where does the resistance to women entering men's jobs actually lie? And when women are admitted, how is a wage differential justified?

Employers may reason that men merit higher salaries (and additional investments in training), or preference in hiring regardless of pay because they will not withdraw for marriage and child-bearing; that men can give more time and effort to the job because they have no domestic responsibilities; that they are more useful because of their greater mobility; that they need more money to support their families. The threat of discontinuity in a woman's worklife is perhaps the greatest single barrier to higher wages for young women. For the older woman, whose children have de-

[24] This issue is raised again in chapter 4.

44

manded her attention in earlier years, the lack of job experience is equally damaging to her earnings potential.

The woman who is considering the occupational options may be discouraged from trying to enter a male's field because she accurately perceives employers' reluctance to hire women for these jobs, or because the investment required of her may exceed her estimate of the return, given her expectation of withdrawal from work for a time, and the uncertainty surrounding her subsequent worklife. She may discount too heavily the future stream of earnings accruing from say, two years of education or training, and thus invest too little in human capital. But perhaps not. For the stream of earnings may not be very high for a woman, and she is well aware of this hazard.

Study might reveal that women have been quite realistic in appraising their potential earnings under different assumptions as to the investment in education, or in many cases that they have erred in the direction of over-investing in education, given the career opportunities that are compatible with their usual lifestyle. It is significant that many women are now challenging that traditional lifestyle by posing some fundamental questions: Why should women assume the obligation for child care? Is it not possible (through day care centers and sharing domestic responsibilities with husbands) for women to have uninterrupted worklives?

Such challenges are the first concerted attempts to remove these major constraints imposed on the market activities of women. To the extent that the efforts bear fruit, and women opt for worklife patterns more nearly like those of men (and those of women in certain other countries, notably Sweden), the career aspirations of women will surely rise, particularly among college-educated women. The impact will likely be felt less on the participation rate of college graduates, which is already high, than on the types of careers women choose. Additional investments of resources in education and job training for women, under these circumstances, would seem to bear high rates of return.

The employment circumstances of college-educated women are far from ideal, however. And these women, being more articulate than women with less education, have repeatedly lodged the complaint of sex discrimination. If these women are the wave of the future, employment patterns may be altered substantially. Salary differentials related to sex will be constantly under scrutiny, and hiring policy even more rigorously policed. Restrictions on entry to higher-level jobs will continue to be attacked. Most of all, those women who not only earn an A.B. but also gain an advanced degree, will continue to argue for improved opportunities in the top professions.

At the moment, no barricade is being stormed with quite as much fervor as the university. There, demands are being made for equal freedom, equal access, equal reward. In particular, the status of the woman professor—her rank, salary, acceptance by peers, visible numbers—is the object of many generalizations and some research. Because it illustrates some of the issues involved in the advancement of women in all professions, the chapter which follows will highlight the issues currently being debated in academic settings across the nation.

3

A Case in Point: Women in the Academic Profession

All of this pitting of sex against sex, of quality against quality; all this claiming of superiority and imputing of inferiority, belongs to the private-school stage of human existence where there are "sides," and it is necessary for one side to beat the other side, and of the utmost importance to walk up to a platform and receive from the hands of the Headmaster himself a highly ornamental pot.

—Virginia Woolf

A common complaint among women with college degrees has to do with the level of work available to them. They point out that they are obliged to take jobs that utilize less than their full intellectual capacities, frequently resorting to secretarial or clerical work which bears little relation to their college training.

Statistics bear out the discrepancy between the educational attainment and the job level of many women. Half the men who work are in the three top occupational groups: managers, officials and proprietors; professional and technical workers; craftsmen and foremen. Only 20 percent of the women are in these top jobs, although they earn 42 percent of all bachelors and first professional degrees. Whereas women make up 37 percent of the labor force, they account for less than 1 percent of the engineers, 2 percent of the executives, 7 percent of the physicians, 15 percent of the salaried managers and officials, and 21 percent of the professionals outside the fields of health and education. The heavy concentration of women in clerical and other service work (which rose from 44 to 50 percent of all women workers in the past decade) is particularly noteworthy.[1]

Of the many professions which educated women enter, the most popular has traditionally been that of teaching. Here, despite a slight increase in the proportion of men going into elementary and secondary education in recent years, the field continues to be dominated by women, perhaps because teaching hours and vacation schedules enable women to work and yet meet the demands of their families. But women's teaching is heavily concentrated at these first two levels; only a very small percentage of all working women continue in school long enough to acquire advanced degrees, and an even smaller proportion hold college or university teaching posts. For those women who do go into higher education, the results are mixed. Perhaps no other profession is now the focus of as much criticism for its alleged discrimination against women.

WOMEN RECIPIENTS OF BACHELOR'S AND ADVANCED DEGREES

During the past decade both the number and the proportion of all bachelor's and first professional degrees earned by women increased significantly. From the turn of the century until the years prior to World War II, women received about 20 percent of these degrees; after the war, the proportion rose sharply, attaining 40 percent in the 1930's and 1940's. In 1950, women's share of first

[1] In contrast, women workers in European countries have come to be less concentrated in clerical work, and educated women apparently have somewhat better representation in certain professions. For example, women make up 7 percent of the physicians in the United States, whereas in Britain they constitute 16 percent, in France 13 percent, and in Germany 20 percent of the total number. Executive positions, too, have larger proportions of women; only 2 percent of these posts are held by women in this country, in contrast with 4 percent in Britain, 9 percent in France, and 12 percent in Germany. Figures cited in *Business in Brief* (Chase Manhattan Bank, October, 1970). Different countries may of course attach different meanings to the term "executive."

48

degrees was down to 24 percent, reflecting the large numbers of male veterans of World War II, who were then graduating. But by 1965 the proportion had again climbed to 41 percent; the 1968 figure was 42 percent.[2] A comparison of the number of college graduations with the number of persons twenty-one years of age in the population reveals the following trends for women and men:[3]

Table 3.1. Graduations as a percent of persons aged 21

	1900	1930	1960	1968
Women	1	4	12	19
Men	3	7	23	26

Changes in proportion of bachelor's and first professional degrees going to women are illustrated by the sex ratio of college graduates. As a recent study from the University of Chicago indicates, women were about one-fourth as likely as men to receive a baccalaurate in 1900. The ratio rose, however, from that 24 percent to 66 percent in 1930, then fluctuated during the abnormal war and postwar era, settling at 56 percent in the mid-1950's. Following a dip in 1958, the figure rose to 71 percent in 1969.[4]

The question of women's dropout rate is frequently raised. Is a woman less likely to enter college or, having entered, less likely to graduate? From the data summarized in the University of Chicago study, it is clear that the college enrollment picture for women has improved substantially in recent decades: 25 percent of female

[2] Data for 1966 and afterwards are not strictly comparable to figures for previous years, because of a change in definition. Specifically, such degrees as M.D., D.D.S., LL.B., B.D., M.L.S., and M.S.W. were previously considered first professional degrees. Starting in 1966, the M.L.S. and the M.S.W. (most of which are taken by women) were reclassified as master's degrees and first professional degrees were specified as those requiring six years or more of higher education. U.S. Department of Labor, Women's Bureau, *Trends in Educational Attainment of Women* (October, 1969), p. 5.

[3] *Ibid.*, p. 5.

[4] *Women in the University of Chicago*, Report of the Committee on University Women (May, 1970), pp. 76–78.

high school graduates entered college in 1939, and 51 percent in 1968. As a percentage of men enrollees, women increased from 59 to 76 percent. Of those men and women entering college, women have tended more frequently to drop out before completing a bachelor's or first professional degree, if one compares the number of degrees conferred with first-time degree-credit college enrollment of four years earlier.[5] However, the completion rate for men has been declining since 1958, and that for women increasing, with the 1967–68 rate for men being 56 percent and that for females 53 percent.

It is when one turns to the data on advanced degrees that he finds the much higher proportion of male recipients. At the level of the master's degree, women's achievement has improved during the past two decades, although still remaining below their relative position in 1930. From 1900, when women received 20 percent of all master's degrees, the proportion rose to 40 percent in 1930, but dropped to 29 percent in 1950, then rose in 1965 to 32 percent. In part as a result of the 1966 change in definition, the 1968 figure rose further to 36 percent.

Trends in the numbers of doctorates earned by women have been similar, with the greatest increases occurring in the first three decades of the century. As a proportion of all doctor's degrees, women received 6 percent in 1900 and 15.4 percent in 1930. Afterwards, the percentage declined to a low of less than 10 percent in 1950. Since 1950, women's share of doctorates has risen to a 1968 figure of almost 13 percent.[6]

WOMEN FACULTY: ACADEMIC RANK AND SALARY

The small proportion of women doctorates suggests that greater attention be directed to the factors which account for women's reluctance or inability to undergo the rigors of graduate education.

[5] Since the first professional degree may require five or more years, figures on completions after four years do not permit firm conclusions as to dropout rates. *Ibid.*, p. 76.

[6] U.S. Department of Labor, *Trends in the Educational Attainment of Women*, Table 5.

Are there barriers to their entrance to graduate schools, and even greater deterrents to the actual completion of advanced degrees? If so, are these barriers imposed by the graduate schools, which choose to ration their scarce resources to men who have better degree-attainment records? Or are there restrictions on the entrance of women to the professions for which graduate education is requisite? Is the record of women's achievement in the academic profession poor enough to discourage young women from undergoing the necessary study? Is it true, as Margaret Mead has argued, that "the academic world is fundamentally hostile, by tradition. . . to those aspects of femininity which involve child bearing" and that, as students and faculty members, academic women must forego their emphasis on such things as personal appearance in favor of interests which are monastic in nature? If so, is this image alone not sufficient to deter women graduates from pursuing an academic profession?

Most of these questions can be answered only in part, despite a raft of recent comments and a few studies of women on college and university faculties.[7] Differences in the attrition rates of men and women graduate students have been explained in various ways: lack of interest and dedication on the part of women; interruption of study by marriage and child-bearing; reluctance of graduate schools to grant fellowship support to women; admissions policies that strongly favor male candidates, particularly after the M.A. degree. Attitudes within graduate departments are highly discriminatory, according to one author,[8] who cites as evidence the higher

[7] See, for example, the selected bibliographies for Ann Sutherland Harris, "The Second Sex in Academe," *AAUP Bulletin*, vol. 56 (1970), p. 295; Patricia Albjerg Graham, "Women in Academe," *Science*, vol. 169 (1970), p. 1290; Martha S. White, "Psychological and Social Barriers to Women in Science," *Science*, vol. 170 (1970), p. 416; and Helen Astin, *The Woman Doctorate in America: Origins, Career, and Family* (New York: Russell Sage Foundation, 1969).

[8] Harris, "The Second Sex in Academe." She offers a series of quotations from various institutions, a few of which follow:

"I know you're competent and your thesis advisor knows you're competent. The question in our minds is are you *really serious* about what you're doing?

grade averages of women entering graduate school at the University of Chicago. The attrition rate in the humanities, moreover, where women typically study, is actually higher for men than women in that institution.

The status of women professors was studied several years ago by Jessie Bernard, who concluded that women held lower ranks and earned lower pay than men and that this generalization held for all types of institutions. On the basis of numbers of publications, she noted that women were less productive than men; as evidence, she cited one study that held age and type of school constant, another that held discipline constant, and still another that held rank and institution constant. In one case she found that among sociologists who received their Ph.D.'s in the 1945–49 period, women were over-represented in the low-productivity brackets and under-represented in the high. To a large proportion of academic women, she concluded, research is less important than teaching.[9]

Salary and academic rank differentials by sex were also reported by the National Education Association, in a survey of the 1965–66 academic market. In that year the median academic year salary for women in all institutions was about 17 percent lower than that for men. Larger differences appeared in the larger universities, within which women on the average earned less than 80 percent of the men's salaries. Women held lower academic rank, and salary differentials existed within these ranks, women's salaries ranging from 91 percent of the men's at the full professor level to 94 percent at the instructor level. Finally, the study confirmed a thesis of Bernard's that women were paid less than men in part because they tended to concentrate in the smaller universities and colleges which

---

"Have you ever thought of Journalism (to a student planning to get a Ph.D. in political science)? I know a lot of women journalists who do very well.

"You're so cute. I can't see you as professor anything.

"Any woman who has got this far has got to be a kook.

"Somehow I can never take women in this field seriously."

[9] Jessie Bernard, *Academic Women* (University Park: Pennsylvania State University Press, 1964), pp. 180–91.

offered lower remuneration to all personnel, albeit especially to women.[10]

In a survey of women doctorates who received their degrees seven to eight years earlier, Helen Astin reported that a third felt they had suffered discrimination in tenure and promotion decisions, and two-fifths in matters of salary.[11] Questioning whether these and other reported instances actually indicate discrimination, the author and a colleague present the results of a study which controls several variables that affect academic rank and salary: education, field, length of time in the labor force, work activity, and work setting.

The findings from the Bayer-Astin study reveal no significant sex differences in rank within major field, academic setting and career length. Through time, however, field differences are apparent: the small number of women in the natural sciences tend toward higher rank than males, whereas the larger number of women in the social sciences tend to hold lower ranks than their male colleagues. In salary, marked sex differences appeared. Women had lower academic salaries across all work settings, fields, and ranks than men who had been teaching the same length of time. Within each category, too, women were paid less than men. Mean salaries for women ranged from 83.8 percent to 98.8 percent of the male mean.[12]

Supporting the authors' conclusion that "the data are suggestive of sex differentials in the academic reward system even when a number of sex- and salary-related contingencies are taken into account" are other reports drawing somewhat broader conclusions. A National Academy of Sciences study of a cohort of doctorates found that it took women longer to achieve full professorships, the time difference being two to five years in the bio-sciences and up to ten in the social sciences. Salary levels for married women

[10] National Education Association, *Research Bulletin*, 44 (May, 1966), pp. 50–57.

[11] Reported in Alan E. Bayer and Helen S. Astin, "Sex Differences in Academic Rank and Salary Among Science Doctorates in Teaching," *Journal of Human Resources*, vol. 3 (1968), p. 192.

[12] *Ibid.*, pp. 198–99.

were 70 to 75 percent of those of men who received their doctorates at the same time. Single women progressed in rank and salary faster than married women, but not as fast as men.[13]

Further instances of sex differences in salary and rank were cited in two other recent journal articles,[14] and a third, although not alleging any discrimination, found that women Ph.D.'s in economics, history, and sociology held lower ranks and earned less pay than men who earned their degrees during the same period, 1958 to 1963. In economics, the average male's salary was about $650 higher than that of the married female's, and $1,100 more than that of the unmarried woman. In sociology the male differential averaged about $1,150, and in history $800. To estimate productivity, three measures were used: numbers of articles published, numbers of books or monographs, and percent having at least one research grant on which the respondent was the chief investigator. The findings indicate higher male productivity in some areas: they had published many more articles and among the historians, men had written more books as well. As to research grants, unmarried women less often had achieved them; married women, however, fared as well as men in two of the three disciplines, sociology and history. The authors point to the fact that married women in these disciplines had higher productivity than the unmarried, and state that this is consistent with the performance of the two groups in physical and natural sciences, social sciences, humanities, and education. They attribute the difference to a selectivity factor; "women who have Ph.D.'s, who have both full-time jobs and homes and children to care for (more than two-thirds of the married women have children) are more achievement-oriented and ambitious than either the unmarried woman Ph.D., or the married man Ph.D."[15]

[13] *Careers of Ph.D.'s, Academic v. Nonacademic, A Second Report on Followups of Doctorate Cohorts, 1935–60* (Washington: National Academy of Sciences), 1968.

[14] Graham, "Women in Academe" and Ann Sutherland Harris, "The Second Sex in Academe."

[15] Rita James Simon and Evelyn Rosenthal, "Profile of the Woman Ph.D. in Economics, History, and Sociology," *AAUW Journal*, vol. 60 (March, 1967), p. 128.

A survey taken by the American Association of University Women found that women were poorly represented in policy-making positions in universities as well as in top-level faculty posts, despite the fact that 90 percent of the responding institutions said that promotion policies were the same for both sexes. In the 450 colleges and universities surveyed, there were on the average 2.6 female department chairmen per institution. About 9 percent of all faculty women were full professors, as compared with 24.5 percent of the faculty men. No institution with over 10,000 students had a woman president; 21 percent of all institutions lacked any women trustees, and another 25 percent had only one. As table 3.2 shows, the proportion of most administrative posts held by women is quite small, except in women's colleges.

The proportion of top leadership posts held by women students is also low. Women are rarely student body presidents or class presidents, for example, in public or private coed institutions. Except for yearbook and literary magazine editors, and (less frequently) newspaper editors and chairmen of activities, women constitute less than one-fifth of any of the major student posts and usually less than one-tenth of the presidencies of classes and student bodies (Table 3.3). Women students have not charged sex discrimination in these choices, however, perhaps because there has been only mild interest in student leadership positions in recent years; to be an officer is in the opinion of many students to be co-opted. There have been charges that some radical student organizations, particularly SDS, have expected women to do the typing and mimeographing, rather than the thinking for the groups.

DEMAND, SUPPLY, AND SEX

Documenting in fine degree the existence of salary and rank differentials in the academic marketplace is perhaps less important then analyzing the bases of these differences. Do the rewards in academic life reflect the fact that the contributions of women and men are somewhat different? One possible explanation for men's higher salaries might be, for example, the greater demand

Table 3.2. Women administrators in colleges and universities, by type of institution, 1970

			Percent who are women in			
Administrative Officers	*Public Colleges*	*Private Colleges*	*Over 10,000 Students*	*Under 1,000 Students*	*Coed Colleges*	*Women's Colleges*
Presidents	3	8	0	13	5	47
Vice-presidents	0	4	0	8	2	17
Directors of development	1	3	0	3	2	6
Business managers	1	9	2	4	5	32
College physicians	9	7	10	5	7	13
Financial aid directors	9	23	12	32	15	67
Placement directors	14	30	10	33	21	73
Counseling directors	9	20	5	32	13	67
Deans of students	9	18	5	26	12	83
Head librarians	22	37	8	62	29	61
Academic deans	8	14	17	15	10	62
Associate or assistant academic deans	11	16	12	20	12	44
Counselors	19	22	16	26	17	51

SOURCE: *Chronicle of Higher Education*, Vol. 5 (November 30, 1970).

Table 3.3. Women student leaders in colleges and universities, by type of institution, 1970

| Student Officers | Percent who are women in | | | | |
	Public Colleges	Private Colleges	Over 10,000	Under 1,000	Coed Colleges
Student body presidents	4	12	2	18	5
Class presidents	8	13	5	22	6
Student union board chairmen	13	15	11	16	12
Debate team captains	13	10	3	8	8
Judicial board chairmen	13	17	6	18	12
Activities committee chairmen	30	31	22	38	27
Freshman orientation chairmen	26	29	28	32	24
Newspaper editors	24	31	18	46	25
Yearbook editors	46	54	48	52	49
Literary magazine editors	23	41	16	63	30

SOURCE: *Chronicle of Higher Education*, Vol. 5 (November, 1970).

for (and hence value attached to) research and writing, as opposed to teaching.

As we noted earlier, Professor Bernard's study indicates that for a large proportion of academic women research is much less significant than teaching. This apparent preference for teaching raises interesting questions and poses a serious dilemma for women in the profession. By and large, women receive their Ph.D.'s from universities that are as good as those from which men take their degrees. But the career pattern thereafter—in particular, the determinative effect of the doctoral university in placing women in jobs—seems to differ, according to Bernard. The institutional placement of women is lower than that of men, and this is true even for unmarried women, who can make independent decisions. Although some of the differential surely results from discrimination, the author points again to the factor of women's preferences.

. . . Academic women constitute a different population, statistically speaking, from academic men. In the world of academic women, career patterns develop along different lines. Women tend to serve in institutions which emphasize different functions, and they themselves are attracted to different kinds of functions. Further, they tend to be in areas which are not in strategic positions in the academic market place and which are not as productive as the areas that attract men.[16]

[16] Bernard, *Academic Women*, p. 92.

To say that women seem to prefer colleges to universities, teaching to research, continued work in one institution to moving around, does not of course tell us why. It is important to ask why. Because if the woman with a Ph.D. from a top-level university goes to and remains in a college because she wants above all to teach undergraduates, the choice is probably a happy one for her, the college, and the students. If, instead, she is being discouraged from competing for university posts where the possible rewards in pay and prestige are greater, because the universities fail to accept her as a competent young scholar, because she fears male competition, or because she thinks of teaching as a more womanly role, then the effect is to allocate talent poorly and to prevent women scholars from realizing their true potential.

But the worst possible set of circumstances evolves when her preference for teaching leads her into a position in which all her time and energy are consumed in teaching and counseling, and as a result she fails to advance in rank and salary because she is "unproductive." The same pattern can be found for men, but it is apparently more frequently the case of women, partly because women seem more often to have teaching preferences. What this suggests is not so much a discrimination against academic women as a failure to give sufficient rewards to teaching. And since women are more often teachers, a larger proportion of them hold lower ranks and salaries.[17]

And what of those women who are research-oriented? Does the academic community reward women for their scientific contributions on the same basis it rewards men? Is it possible for women to make comparable contributions, given the limited opportunities for interaction with colleagues, the weakness of the protege system in fostering women's professional advance, and the general exclusion of women from the scientific-social dialogue? Martha White's analysis of the identity problems of professional women is a compelling one.[18] Granted that defense of a thesis turns in the final analysis on the supporting evidence; that scientific findings

[17] Juanita M. Kreps, "Sex and the Scholarly Girl," *AAUP Journal*, vol. 51 (March, 1965), pp. 30–33.
[18] White, "Psychological and Social Barriers," pp. 414–16.

58

are not a function of the sex of the investigator; that a woman re-searcher has access to the same body of fact and theory, and is subject to the same constraints imposed by gaps in information; that she, too, must piece together, interpolate, guess, but even-tually subject her conclusions to the cold scrutiny of colleagues and editors; nevertheless, a woman does suffer some exclusion from that information stored in men's minds, and her research may suffer accordingly. Of course it is possible that being out of the mainstream merely keeps one's mind free of the trade gossip.

But there is a prior condition for woman's success in the aca-demic profession or any other that requires lengthy preparation or heavy investment in human capital). That condition is a will-ingness on her part and that of society to forego earnings and to expend significant educational resources with the thought that sub-sequently a high rate of return will ensue. Investments in a male's professional future are seldom challenged; barring premature death, his lifetime earnings will compensate him handsomely for extending his education. For a woman, future earnings are far less predictable. Unless she is willing to foreswear marriage and chil-dren, she faces interruptions in earnings, possibly for several years, and the probable need for some later retraining to get back into her profession. In many disciplines knowledge erodes rapidly and the value of an advanced degree is dependent, in large part, on when it was earned.

Thus it is not difficult to understand the reluctance of women to take a chance on themselves; certainly it is easy to understand the societal stance that investments in the male's education bears a more certain return, on the average. The wonder may be, not that we produce so few women who make the investment, but that we produce so many. For the supply of women aspiring to academic careers is now increasing, their salary and professional rank relative to those of men notwithstanding. The growth in num-bers of women entering the field is perhaps due to the scarcity of other attractive alternatives. Or, stated positively, college teaching apparently continues to offer one of the best combinations of sal-ary, working hours and conditions, and intellectual challenge open to women.

Unfortunately, a major problem confronting all academic personnel during the 1970's is that of job availability. In contrast to the past two decades when the demand for teachers seemed insatiable, our projected supply of teachers will exceed the expected demand during the coming decade. It will be possible to absorb much larger numbers of Ph.D.'s in academic jobs, of course, if society feels it can afford higher quality higher education, or higher education for a larger proportion of the relevant age group. The fact that we have passed the peak numbers in the college age group need not signal a decline (or even a leveling-off) in the numbers of professors employed. But since conditions in the profession will depend to such a great extent on the state of demand, it is difficult to predict the outcome of present pressures on university administrations to hire more women faculty members; to guarantee equal treatment in salary, rank and tenure; to provide more assistance to women graduate students, thereby enabling them to earn Ph.D. degrees.

The aggregate numbers of new degrees will be only one of the factors at issue; equally important is the question of the fields of study. Will more women move into the natural sciences, engineering, mathematics, and economics, or will they continue to study history, English literature, Romance languages and sociology? If the former, they will join male-dominated disciplines, where the barriers are perhaps (and the pay certainly) greater. If the latter, their acceptance is assured by tradition. But precisely because they have been accepted the supply of talented women has been great, and salaries have been pushed down. Salary differentials between disciplines reflect in part the heavier preponderance of women in certain fields. The reluctance of women to storm other barricades may now be weakening, as a result of the overall push for women's rights. What we do not know is the extent of women's interests in the future in areas other than the humanities.

MARKET FORCES AND INSTITUTIONAL BIAS

If the demand for college professors slows further and the number of job applicants substantially exceeds the numbers being hired at going rates of pay, the sex of the job seeker may become even more important in the hiring process. The pressure to give scarce jobs to men because they have families to support, sometimes cited and accepted as a rationale in earlier periods, will be counterbalanced somewhat, however, by the current concern with equal rights for women.

A downward movement in the demand for certain groups of workers may point up some sex-related differences we have not witnessed during recent years. When jobs are expanding, an employer is prompted to reach farther and farther down the labor queue, hiring workers in the order of their attractiveness to him. Which potential employee he finds attractive depends on his own mind-set as well as the characteristics of the persons in line. The sex of the applicant is an important characteristic, so important for many jobs that only one sex is acceptable. Members of the other sex are then so far down the line they have little chance of being employed in that job; in effect, they constitute a different line altogether.

One beauty of a tight labor market lies in the gradual acceptance of those persons in the second line who thenceforth can be considered on the basis of individual competence, rather than generalized preconception. Thus the major breakthroughs for women in the work force have occurred during periods of excess demand for labor; World War II is an example. Employers, "resorting" to women workers during the quarter of a century following that war, have opened new career opportunities for women who, once employed in sufficient numbers, have never gone back to the noncompeting line.

But what happens if the labor market softens? In which jobs are women now accepted on an equal footing with men? In particular, have women applicants for academic posts advanced in the queue to the point where they compete with their male colleagues on the basis of their individual capabilities? And even if their competence qualifies them for a job, will the institution waive its concern for supporting the man with a family?

To all these questions, the answer may be yes. Many colleges and universities would protest the questions, in fact, on the basis that they are when-did-you-stop-beating-your-wife inquiries. Still, the salary and rank differentials have existed and in a period of excess demand. When market forces make it necessary to cut back or to hire fewer new instructors, how much significance will the sex of the applicants assume? Within the construct of the market for academic talent, some reordering of applicants is not at all unlikely. Women could be hired more readily because from the roles of those applying they are more competent and there is no bias against females; because they are willing to teach heavier loads or accept less pay; because they are slower to demand promotion and tenure. If universities begin to emphasize undergraduate teaching at the expense of research, women may find their job opportunities improved vis-a-vis those of men.

The difficult research problem is that of separating the impact of market demand for a particular occupational group—in this instance, professors—from any discriminatory practices on the part of the employer. Analysis of academic placements needs to take into account any aggregate shift in demand, as well as the differential effect of this shift on men and women instructors— effects which may be felt in numbers hired, compensation, teaching loads, etc. The time dimension is critical. When a cohort of male and females receiving their Ph.D.'s in, say, 1970, is followed for several years, market forces can be assumed to have affected all of them in roughly the same manner. Differences in salaries and academic rank, by sex, can then be isolated, as can continuity of teaching, research productivity, contributions to professional organizations, etc. It might be discovered that married professional women lag behind men in performance on any of these criteria because of the break in career their children occasion. In that case, the relevant comparison would be between a cohort of women and the next younger cohort of men. The necessity of making this type of comparison suggests an inequity; the only offset, perhaps, is the woman's advantage of having a longer life expectancy, which might enable her to "catch up" by extending her career to a later age. But alas, retirement policies allow comparatively little work flexibility in the latter part of life!

4

The Value of Women's Work

> Middle-class and upper-class women can depend on income
> that bears no direct connection to their efforts, ability, or out-
> put. They have achieved, in effect, a guaranteed annual wage.
> They receive it because of their ascriptive status—wife. This
> definition is upheld by the social system; for example, in di-
> vorce actions, alimony for the wife is often calculated on the
> basis of the style of life her husband has provided her with be-
> fore the separation.
>
> —Cynthia Fuchs Epstein

The reasons for married women's recent increase in labor force
participation are complex, as the preceding questions have indicated. Glen Cain has drawn attention to the problem of separating those factors that influence the wife's decision to join the labor
force from those which merely reflect her decision to do so. Other
authors have raised specific questions: to what extent have labor-
saving devices freed women from household work, leading them
to look for paying jobs to occupy their time, and to what extent
have women's decision to work for pay made such appliances
necessary, and financed their purchase? Does the recent downturn
in the birthrate, made possible by newer contraceptive methods,
reflect high career aspirations on the part of this generation of
women? Or, having decided to have smaller families, do women

63

in their mid-thirties then find themselves with so few demands on their time that they flee an empty home for a crowded job market?

As previous study shows, the major variables affecting a married woman's decision to enter or reenter the labor force are her age, her educational attainment, and her husband's income. Additional factors such as the number of children, place of residence, race, husband's attitude, religious beliefs, etc., are either taken into account in the first three variables, or are relatively insignificant in influencing female labor force participation. The thesis cited in chapter 3, that it has been primarily the growth in demand for female workers that has brought about the growth in the proportion of married women who work, assumes a willingness on the part of these females to change the nature of their activities from home work to market work, as the latter becomes available.

THE ECONOMICS OF MARKET-NONMARKET WORK DECISIONS WITHIN THE FAMILY

Such a willingness clearly exists for great numbers of women. How many of them elect to take jobs (or stated differently, what it takes to induce any given number to take jobs) depends upon their evaluation of two sets of advantages: the home set, consisting of more time for leisure, hobbies, and community activity; closer attention to the needs of the family; economies reaped through full attention to home management; freedom of schedule, etc.; and the market set, including earnings and fringe benefits; job status; associations available in the work place; interest in the work itself.

In weighing these two sets of alternatives, the need for income is an overriding consideration for a very large percentage of women. Of the thirty million women now at work, more than twelve million are single, divorced, separated or widowed. Many of these women are the sole source of support not only for themselves but for children or parents as well. In addition, almost five million of the working women are married to men who earn less than $5,000 annually. Thus more than half the women in the labor force do not have the luxury of choosing home work over market work;[1] in fact, there can be little doubt that the relatively low participation rate of women with low educational achievement is due to their lack of job opportunities. If jobs were available to these women, the market set of advantages would surely win over the nonmarket.

For families on very low incomes, the wage necessary to induce the wife to take a job is also low, since the value of each additional dollar of income has high utility. As the husband's income rises, we observe that the wife's willingness to join the labor force declines, other things equal; the supply of wives' market services is thus a backward-bending curve when correlated with husbands' incomes (Figure 2.1). We know little, however, about the market behavior of wives in relation to their own possible range of earnings, beyond the fact that the higher their educational achievement (and hence their potential earnings), the more likely they are to work. Moreover, Mincer's conclusion that the increase in wives' labor force participation through time could be explained by the rise in their own earnings, which more than offset the negative effects of their husband's rise in incomes, would seem to indicate that married women respond positively to wage incentives.

The degree of this responsiveness to wage incentive turns on the perceived value of the alternative use of the wife's time. In the absence of information on the value a family places on the wife's nonmarket services, the elasticity of married women's labor supply is difficult to estimate. It is clear that their supply (and that of other groups of secondary workers) is more elastic than that of primary workers. The reason for this greater elasticity is important to note, although it is of course self-evident: men's alternative to market work is free time, which may or may not have utility, whereas a wife's alternatives are free time and nonmarket work, the latter having utility in most instances. Thus when a man goes to work, no loss in value is imputed to the free time he gives

[1] For further discussion see Elizabeth D. Koontz, "Not Just for Pin Money," U.S. Department of Labor, Women's Bureau, June, 1970.

up. On the contrary, any loss in time from work is considered a loss in income, or foregone earnings. But married women's non-market services are of value; problems of analysis arise from the fact that we do not know, household to household, precisely what value.

The maximum value placed on a nonworking wife's services can be deduced from the salary that does in fact induce her to take a job. Similarly, there is some theoretical minimum below which wives at work will withdraw from their jobs, and devote their time to home work. The asking price is higher, the greater the value attached to home work and this value obviously varies at different stages of a family's life cycle, each stage making a different set of demands on the wife's time. Between families in the same stage, however, the values also differ; the presence of children in Negro families has been less of a deterrent to the wife's market work than children have been in white families, where the need for income was less pressing. For any given family size and age composition, the relative value imputed to the wife's home work is obviously lower, the greater the perceived need for additional income.

WIVES' NONMARKET WORK AND THE
CONCEPT OF OPPORTUNITY COSTS

Since we do not place a price on wives' nonmarket work, no value for these services enters the national income accounts. We do add in the value of their services when they take jobs, however. The Gross National Product is thus increased by the salaries earned, with no reduction for the loss of home work. Through time, a rise in the market participation of wives increases the dollar value of the national product more than the net gain in services warrants. More specifically, the value of the national product is overstated by the value of wives' foregone nonmarket services. Were the participation rate to decline, moreover, GNP would show only the loss in market income, although wives would then perform many services for the family that formerly were not rendered, or had to be purchased in the market.[2]

The components to be included in the calculation of the national product were initially indicated in Alfred Marshall's *Principles of Economics*, where the services which families perform for themselves were excluded from the accounts. Since that time, however, the practice of imputing a dollar value to agricultural commodities produced and consumed by the family, and to owner-occupied dwellings, has been adopted. There have been discussions of including also in the national product an imputed value of unpaid housework,[3] but none have led to action.

The National Bureau of Economic Research estimated that the value of housewives' services amounted to one-fourth the amount of the gross national product in 1918, and a decade later Simon Kuznets found a value of slightly over one-fourth the GNP. In the 1930's Swedish economists suggested including a value for domestic work performed by wives and daughters, based on wages paid to domestic servants. Colin Clark estimated the value of unpaid household services for industrialized societies, and indicated a method of imputing such a value.[4] He deplored the fact that we continue to ignore such work in the computations of national product, and his view is supported by other economists. Gardner Ackley notes that "not to recognize the value of these productive

[2] In *The Economics of Welfare*, A. C. Pigou cites the classic example:
"If a number of bachelors who were employing housekeepers in the customary manner of exchanging services for money, decided to marry these housekeepers, then the national dividend would be diminished! Obviously the housekeeper, when assuming the role of wife, regardless of any additional services she assumed by virtue of her marriage, continued to perform those services which she, as a housekeeper, had been performing previously. In others words, the services continued but the value disappeared!"

[3] This review of attempts to include an imputed value for housework and estimates of this value is drawn from an address by Sylva M. Gelber, "The Labour Force; the GNP; and Unpaid Housekeeping Services," Canada Department of Labour, Ottawa, June, 1970.

[4] Colin Clark, "The Economics of Housework," *Bulletin of the Oxford Institute of Statistics*, vol. 20 (May, 1958).

services is a source of serious bias in the national product."[5] A 1968 estimate of the value of housewives' services again placed the total at about one-fourth of the GNP.[6]

Attempts to impute a dollar value to nonmarket work done by wives are hampered by a lack of data on the prices of many services which are typically performed primarily in the home, and by our inability to attach monetary values to certain intangible qualities usually associated with having a wife and mother in the home: companionship, attention, interest in the family's welfare, continuity of relationship with young children. An alternative approach is to estimate the opportunity costs of the wife's home work by supposing that its value equals the foregone earnings in the labor market. Although this method would leave many of the vital questions unattended, it would nevertheless allow us to take into account *some* value for nonmarket work, thereby reducing the degree of overstatement in output that occurs when women enter market jobs.

The development and publicizing of such an accounting procedure would not only improve the measure of growth in real output; it might also change the attitudes of women toward market and nonmarket work. On the current scene, one of the most frequently cited complaints of women is the fact that they are expected to do routine, repetitive household chores, for which there is no monetary reward. They are frequently eager to trade this work for a market job which may be equally routine and repetitive; the difference is that the market job pays a salary. Imputing a dollar value to home work would not make it more rewarding of course; it might make it seem so. An actual payment to wives for such services is not as absurd as might appear at first glance. The important question is whether the society wants labor resources allocated to home work (and leisure) or to market work.

[5] Gardner Ackley, *Macroeconomic Theory* (New York: Macmillan, 1961), p. 55.

[6] See Miss Gelber's reference to Ahmad Hussein Shamseddine, *The Economics and Business Bulletin* (Philadelphia: Temple University, 1968).

The rough estimates of the opportunity costs of wives' nonmarket work, which follow, indicate one method of approach, but more importantly, they indicate the data needed for an accurate appraisal of the gains and losses that may be occasioned by changes in wives' labor force status.

Housework done by wives

American women, especially married ones, do most of the housework. James Morgan and his associates estimate that married women spend an average of forty hours per week in this endeavor.[7] Adding these hours to those which women spend in market work gives a total workweek in excess of that reported by male heads of families (Figure 4.1). The wife typically did 2,053 hours of unpaid household work in a year.

Hourly earnings of wives who work

Sirageldin's estimates of the hourly earnings of wives who worked in 1964, by age and educational groups, are shown in Table 4.1. Age and education were the major determinants of the rate earned, the range being from an average of $1.14 per hour for wives aged eighteen to twenty-four with less than twelve grades of school completed, to $3.50 per hour for those aged 45–54 with college degrees.

Annual earnings of wives

Average hourly earnings are translated into annual salaries (at the 2,053 hours per year estimated by Morgan, *et al.*) in Table 4.2. Again, the range was wide: from $2,340 per year to $7,186. The opportunity cost for a thirty-year-old housewife to remain at home engaged in housework was $2,566 if she had less than

---

[7] Morgan, Sirageldin, and Baerwaldt, *Productive Americans*, p. 102. The authors also note that women do 70 percent of all housework done by family members.

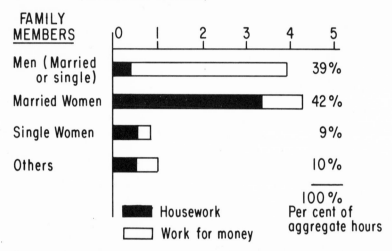

Figure 4.1 AGGREGATE HOURS OF REGULAR HOUSEWORK
AND WORK FOR MONEY DONE BY VARIOUS
FAMILY MEMBERS IN 1964
(in millions of hours)

Source: Morgan, Sirageldin, and Boerwaldt. op. cit., p. 103

twelve years of education, or $5,892 if she had a college degree; a fifty-year-old wife with a college degree was foregoing $7,186; and so on. The opportunity cost of women's services is highest in the forty-five to fifty-four year age group for those with less than twelve years of school or with college degrees; for the high school graduate, the cost is highest in the thirty-five to forty-four age bracket.

Sirageldin estimates that the average value of unpaid output for the American family was $3,929, or about fifty percent of its disposable income, in 1964.[8] Approximately ninety percent of this estimated production was in the form of housework, giving a value

[8] Sirageldin, *Non-Market Components*, p. 53.

70

Table 4.1. Hourly earnings of wives by age and educational groups, 1964

Education	Less than 12 Grades	12 Grades but no College	College Degree
Age			
18–24	$1.14	$1.48	$3.12
25–34	1.25	2.00	2.87
35–44	1.42	1.99	2.91
45–54	1.67	1.66	3.50
55–64	1.55	1.96	2.70
65+	1.14	1.48	2.50

SOURCE: Sirageldin, Non-Market Components, p. 31.

of $3,536 for housework per family. As figure 4.1 shows, married women do most of this work—about ten times as many hours per week as married men.

Numbers of nonworking wives

Given the rough indicators of opportunity costs for women not in the labor force, as indicated in Table 4.2, we raise the question: what would be the effect on GNP if all the nonworking wives (aged eighteen and over) without children of preschool age came to be employed in market jobs?

Table 4.2. Opportunity cost of non-labor force activity of wives, by age and educational groups, 1964

Age	Less than 12 grades	12 Grades but no college	College degree
18–24	$2,340	$3,038	$6,405
25–34	2,566	4,016	5,892
35–44	2,915	4,085	5,974
45–54	3,429	3,408	7,186
55–64	3,182	3,924	5,543
65+	2,340	3,038	5,133

SOURCE: Calculated from Sirageldin, *Non-Market Components*, and Morgan, Sirageldin, and Baerwaldt, *Productive Americans*.

Table 4.3, taken from Oppenheimer's estimates, indicates the size of the pools of potential female workers in 1960. Not counting the single, widowed, and divorced women, the total number of married women who remained outside the labor force and who could theoretically have taken jobs, was almost 26 million. This figure excludes married women with children of pre-school age.

Table 4.3.   Pools of potential female workers: 1960

(in thousands)

Category	Number
Single women 18–34[a]	3,284
Women 18–34 unmarried and married with husbands absent	4,853
Women 18–34, except for married women (husband present) with pre-school-age children	8,950
Married women 18–34 (husband present) except for those with pre-school-age children	5,676
Single, widowed, and divorced women 18–64	10,311
Women 18–64, unmarried and married with husbands absent	12,565
Women 18–64, except for married women (husbands present) with pre-school-age children	36,133
Married women 18–64 (husbands present) except for those with pre-school-age children	25,822

[a] Girls 18–19 years old enrolled in school are omitted in all categories.

SOURCE: Oppenheimer, *Female Labor Force*, p. 172.

Aggregate cost of foregone earnings

In Table 4.4, we show rough estimates of the earnings that might have accrued to various age and educational groups of married women not then employed, had they been in market jobs in 1960.[9] These very tentative results indicate, for example, that if all forty-five to fifty-four year-old married women who had college degrees and who were engaged in nonmarket activities had been employed in paying jobs, their total earnings would have

[9] The 1964 opportunity costs for each age and educational group (the opportunity cost per person shown in Table 4.2, times the numbers of wives in each age-educational group as indicated by Oppenheimer's percentages, noted in footnote a, Table 4.4) are deflated to the 1960 figure on the basis of the 1964 index of hourly compensation in the total private economy.

Table 4.4. **Estimated aggregate costs of foregone earnings of married women by age and educational group, 1960**

(in millions)

Education	Less than 12 grades[a]	12 Grades but no college[a]	College Degree[a]	Rate of non-participation
Age Group				
18–24	$11,766	$ 2,328	$ 3,273	71.5
25–34	12,639	3,015	2,885	72.1
35–44	11,823	3,888	3,108	63.5
45–54	23,783	3,513	5,025	60.7
55–64	14,022	2,594	2,449	74.8
65+	2,058	482	543	93.2
Total[b]	71,709	15,819	17,283	69.4

[a] Based on Oppenheimer's estimate that 80 percent of the total female labor force has received twelve grades or less of education; 12.1 percent has twelve grades of school; and 7.9 percent has four years or more of college (p. 82).

[b] The summation of the totals for the three educational categories yields a figure of $104.8 billion, as compared with the $107 billion estimated on the basis of the *average* value of unpaid output attributable to household activity.

SOURCE: Calculated from Sirageldin, *Non-Market Components*; Oppenheimer, *Female Labor Force*; and Tables 4.2 and 4.3.

been over five billion dollars. Similarly, if all twenty-five to thirty-four year-old nonworking married women with up to 12 years of education had been engaged in market activity, their earnings would have been three billion dollars. The foregone earnings of married women in all age and educational groups total roughly $105 billion; this addition would have raised the 1960 GNP of $622.6 by over one-sixth.

MAXIMUM CONTRIBUTION OR MAXIMUM PAY?

Many questions can be raised regarding the foregoing calculations, not the least of which are questions of the method and the validity of the data used. The use of average hourly earnings for women of any particular group, rather than some sort of declining marginal wage as women are added to the labor force, will offend economists. We have used the pools of potential female workers in 1960, and made only a rough correction for wage changes

73

backward from 1964 to 1960. A more reliable dollar estimate of the value of wives' home work could be made, based perhaps on 1970 census data.

In defense of the proposition that an improved estimate would add an important dimension to our thinking, one has only to raise some larger questions regarding the effect on the welfare of the family and society from increasing labor force participation of married women. Despite our protests that growth in income is not to be equated with improvements in welfare; that society places a high value on the services of wives in the home and in the community; that the absence of a price tag on a particular service does not render it valueless—despite these caveats, the tendency to identify one's worth with the salary he earns is a persistent one. This tendency is not peculiar to men who earn salaries; it pervades as well the thinking of women who work at unpaid jobs.

Within the family, where the market work-nonmarket work decision is made, a seemingly low value placed on home work may make the pay offered by an ordinary market job very appealing to the wife. If the resulting effect is a shift of more and more wives into the labor force, the aggregate growth in national income confirms the societal view that the contribution made by wives was low, but increases as they go into the job market. In the microeconomic setting, nonmarket activities are likely to be undervalued and in the macro they are valued at zero.

In her proposal that housewives running their homes be included in the statistics of the active labor force, and in the benefits that accrue to members of the labor force, Sylva Gelber of the Canada Department of Labour cites the gains wives would make, even in the absence of money payments for housework: social security entitlements (such as pension accumulations) would be conferred for the years of work at home; allowances provided under the Adult Retraining Programme, now available to persons attached to the labor force for at least three years, would be available; a more positive attitude toward the value of domestic work on the part of both society and the housewife would ensue. "Belittling of the role of housewife . . . has been responsible, in no small part, for many of the dissatisfactions being experienced at the present time, particularly by some younger women. . . ."[10]

It is well to raise the question of whether wives would be entering the labor force in their present numbers, if they earned salaries for doing home work (or even if they were made conscious of the opportunity cost of that work). An even more basic question has to do with wives' contributions to welfare in their alternative functions: when does an increase in the labor force participation of married women improve welfare? If it seemed socially desirable to encourage mothers of young children to stay in the home, would the payment of a salary for the work not serve that end? The present public assistance arrangement for aid to dependent children is somewhat comparable, but it is available only in the absence of other family income and it is viewed as a dole, rather than a payment for work performed.

When some work pays a wage or salary and other work does not, it is difficult for the family or for society to compare by reference to a dollar measure the relative values of the two types of work. The activity which is rewarded with a pay check is likely to be valued more highly in our society, with the not unusual result that women may strive to maximize their dollar earnings, which may or may not maximize their contribution to family welfare. For women who have no option as to whether they will seek jobs—female heads of households, mothers of children in poor families, etc.—the social costs of enforced market activity may be higher in the long run than the costs of providing family income in *lieu* of market work.

These are of course two separate issues. In the first instance, women are drawn into the job market because of a systematic undervaluing of their services in the home; in the latter, women are forced into market work regardless of the value they place on the alternative use of their time at home. But payment for nonmarket work—whether or not it could be instituted—would affect both situations: it would improve the information base for decision-making in the first case, and provide a market-nonmarket work option in the second.

[10] Gelber, *Labour Force*, p. 4.

5

Home and Market Work in Lifetime Perspective

> A young boy knows that he will have to work when he grows up. If one asks a boy of five what he wants to be, he will reply in terms of an occupation—aviator, fireman, doctor. He will not answer that he will be "a daddy." But if his sister is asked, she is likely to say that when she grows up, she will be "a mommy." Each is considered an acceptable response.
>
> —Eli Ginzberg

The amount of the overstatement of GNP that has accompanied the secular rise in women's labor force participation rates depends in part on how the nonmarket work once done by nonworking wives gets to be done when wives go into market jobs. Is leisure time simply traded for money income, or does previous nonmarket activity now become market activity as housework is done commercially? The exclusion of free time from the income accounts means that any market activity replacing it appears as a net gain in the national product; in this respect, a reduction in free time and a reduction in nonmarket work are treated in the same manner. Conversely, the long-run decline in the length of the workweek, the lengthening of vacation time, etc., have the effect of understating the rate of economic growth. De Grazia has argued that leisure time has not been increasing significantly if at all, even though the number of hours of market work has declined, since husbands must now help do the nonmarket work formerly done by wives.[1]

The tradeoff between leisure and market work on the part of the primary worker is different, nevertheless, from that between market and nonmarket work for the wife in at least one respect: the latter requires major changes in the family's lifestyle, reducing (perhaps eliminating altogether) the wife's time free of work. Since most women who work have full-time jobs, and since the amount of domestic service is decreasing, we know that most wives who work are doing two jobs. Data cited in the preceding chapter reinforce the conclusion that wives continue to do most of the work in the home. A large part of women's current discontent with housework can surely be attributed to society's expectation that they meet this domestic obligation, regardless of the demands of their market jobs—a career constraint not imposed upon men. An increasing proportion of married women thus find themselves in conflict with the domestic role they are expected to play, frustrated in their attempts to give adequate attention to their families and at the same time develop their own careers.

HOME WORK: AN OCCUPATION OF CEREMONIAL FUTILITY?

This conflict is not a new one; it merely requires a new answer. Throughout the past several decades of growing interest in the female labor force, the solution offered would-be career women has been: don't marry, or at least don't have children. But of course women have continued to do both since both seemed to be perfectly normal things to do, and in any case they usually made their commitments before they were mature enough to understand the limits that marriage and children imposed. Once a woman has a family, little advice is offered beyond the usual reminders that any career she has should be tailored to fit her primary

---

[1] Sebastian de Grazia, *Of Time, Work, and Leisure* (New York: Twentieth Century Fund, 1962).

responsibilities. There is a noticeable silence on the subject of the constraints families place on husbands' careers. In short, many women feel that having a family should no more exclude them from careers than it does men, and they are suddenly willing to make rather a point of the whole thing.

Many writers, male and female, have argued that technology has done women out of their traditional functions: growing and preparing food, making clothing, nursing children. Advertisers clearly believe that there is some truth in this argument, for by their interpretation married women are now driven to a pathological concern with whiter clothes and shinier floors, which serve as antiseptic substitutes for the large and demanding families of the past. But the huckster's perception of today's woman is not necessarily realistic. Women's higher levels of education and intelligence have led to higher aspirations for children, to greater concern for the physical and emotional health of all members of the family, to concern with community programs that replace many earlier home-bound activities.

Women's interest in having careers is not from their lack of family responsibilities; family care is far from the occupation of ceremonial futility that Veblen alleged. It is in fact the central importance of this function that makes work outside the home impossible for many women and unsatisfactory for many others. For if indeed the work of being wife and mother were minimal, the pursuit of career interests would pose no problem. And if the woman's responsibilities to her family could be met altogether within the home, even this might reduce the friction.

But today's wife and mother is obliged to know a great deal about society in order to serve adequately the family's needs. The interests she needs to develop in the course of rearing children are quite broad if not scholarly. It is no male feat that children's education has been improving rapidly in recent decades, nor is it the accomplishment of spinster schoolteachers. We educate women well for the very good reason that they are more or less in charge of the education of all other persons, save adults. A problem arises, however, when women turn to apply their education beyond the home, and this is true even when many of the family's needs can be met only with knowledge of, and a keen interest in, matters outside the home. If society educated women less well, many of their current complaints would not have emerged; in the case of women it is not a little knowledge, but a good bit, that is a dangerous thing—dangerous, that is, to traditional work patterns.

What we discovered quite some time ago was the wisdom of opening to women the same educational opportunities that were available to men. But in that earlier time it also suited our convenience to have a sexual division of labor that served the interests of the family, and woman's role (or at least one of the roles) had to be carried on within the home. But it *was* merely a convenience and it did serve only that more primitive stage in economic development. We have now to find a way to accommodate the family's much broader range of needs and interests. These needs exceed the capabilities of the home itself; in reality, this has been the case for some time. Women's heavy schedule of community activities is the evidence.

Future Labor Force Activity of Married Women

Since work in the home no longer satisfies either the family's expanding goals or the wife's growing interests, it would seem likely that wives' market work would continue to grow, with higher and higher proportions of married women becoming labor force participants. Two questions emerge: first, will the future occupational composition of the labor force be such that women workers will more easily find jobs? And second, from which groups of presently nonworking women will any new participants be drawn? The first of these questions was introduced in Chapter 2, as part of the broader question of the demand for college-educated women workers. It is important to return to this issue, to examine the relationship between the projected labor force needs and the expected supply of all occupational classes of women workers.

Labor Force Projections to 1980

In line with past developments, we would expect the increase in female labor force activity to depend in large measure on the economy's growth in demand for jobs typically performed by women. Figure 5.1 shows the expected percentage increases in numbers of persons employed in several occupations, including

Figure 5.1. Growth in selected occupations, projected to 1980 (as a percent of numbers in 1968)

	0–25%	25–50%	50–75%	75–100%	100% or more
All occupations		37[a]			
All professional and technical occupations			35		
Systems analysts					40
Programmers					40
Psychologists				30	
Medical laboratory workers[b]				85	
Physicians			10		
Registered nurses			100		
Social workers			65		
Clerical workers			70		
Engineers		1			
Natural scientists		15			
College and University teachers		25			
Engineering and science technicians		13			
Elementary school teachers	75				
Secondary school teachers	75				
Service workers[c]	60				

[a] Percentage of women currently employed in the occupation.

[b] Includes technologists, technicians, and aides.

[c] Includes domestic maids, hospital attendants, practical nurses, nurses aides, restaurant workers, beauty operators, janitors, and building cleaners.

SOURCE: *Manpower Report of the President, 1970; Monthly Labor Review*, June, 1970; *Handbook of Women Workers, 1969.*

some of the ones that have been dominated by women in the past. The proportion of the jobs in each occupation held by women is indicated by the number at the end of each line.

The pattern of expected growth in the traditional women's jobs is mixed. Of the seven occupations dominated by women (i.e., 50 percent or more of the workers are female), only one—medical laboratory workers, 85 percent of whom are women—will be a very high-growth occupation. Registered nurses who are all women, and clerical and social workers, who are mainly women, will also see high rates of increase in the 1970's. But the numbers of elementary and secondary school teachers, another female group, will have a rate of growth significantly lower than the average for all occupations, and only about one-third of the rate for all professional and technical occupations. Service workers, of whom 60 percent are women, will also see only a small increase in numbers. Of the total numbers of workers in the fastest-growing occupations, systems analysts and programmers, about 40 percent were women in 1968.

Although these projections indicate a continuing demand for the jobs women have traditionally done, it is clear that women will need to make some important shifts in their occupational choices if they are to take advantage of certain areas of rapid expansion. Computer programming may well replace elementary school teaching as a major vocation of women college graduates; in fact, women may come to dominate in this new field to the same degree they now staff secretarial, clerical, and most other office jobs. So far, however, the concentration of women in a few jobs has persisted.[2]

Which Pool of Female Labor?

Janice Hedges has drawn attention to the fact that women with quite different characteristics are now at work:

. . . As first one group of women then another entered (black women and immigrants were the pioneers, followed by young women and

[2] Janice N. Hedges, "Women Workers and Manpower Demands in the 1970's," *Monthly Labor Review*, vol. 93 (June, 1970), pp. 19–29.

single women, then "mature" women, and currently, mothers of pre-school children), every major group has been encompassed. In 1969, women who worked bore a marked resemblance to those who stayed at home as to marital status, age, education and other characteristics.[3]

In figure 5.2, the author shows the relatively small differences between the percentages of women in various categories of the population, and those in the labor force. It is clearly no longer possible to distinguish the working woman as one who is married or unmarried, young or old, black or white, or even as one with or without young children. The working pattern is an all-pervasive one.

The potential supply of female labor appears to lack the major untapped groups available in earlier decades. In contrast to the situation that prevailed when most females in the labor force were young women, the 1950's and 1960's saw the influx of older women, which gave the participation curve the familiar M shape. Of the age groups now left to draw from, the largest group is comprised of women who are in the trough of the curve—that stage in the women's lives when their children are born and reared to school age. But as figure 1.1 shows, the 1970 dropout from work is not as pronounced as the one for 1960 (and the whole 1970 curve lies far above the 1960 one), indicating that the pool of nonworking women with small children is diminishing.

Such analyses of the participation rate for women of different ages at a point in time are not satisfactory in explaining the labor force behavior of any group of women as they progress through their life course. Cohort analysis—studies that show the patterns for a series of cohorts, at different stages in the life cycle—allow the researcher some insight into those characteristics which are due to the particular stage of the woman's life, as opposed to those that arise from the societal circumstances of her particular generation. Matilda Riley has used the cohort approach to call into question the woman's "typical" work-life pattern. She points out that only one of the cohorts—the one born in the decade 1886 to 1895—actually observes the pattern usually ascribed to women.

[3] *Ibid.*, p. 21.

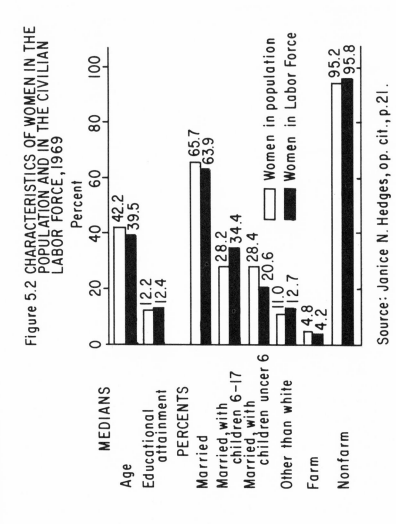

Figure 5.2 CHARACTERISTICS OF WOMEN IN THE POPULATION AND IN THE CIVILIAN LABOR FORCE,1969

Source: Janice N. Hedges, op. cit., p.21.

83

The next cohort does not withdraw from the labor force as early as age fifty, and the two subsequent ones show no tendency to withdraw during the child-bearing period. Rather, there is now emerging a picture of rising participation through the life course.[4] The author emphasizes a point made by Bruno Bettleheim (Chapter 2): women have always worked; the only question is that of the type of work performed. Except perhaps for a brief period during the twentieth century, women have not considered housekeeping and child-rearing full-time activities.

Whatever withdrawals from the labor force that occur now will surely be decreased by the appearance of child-care facilities that reduce the need for mothers to leave their jobs. Such facilities have never received high priority in this country, perhaps because the supply of women workers has usually been adequate and there has been no need for measures designed to aid in their recruitment. Interest in providing day-care for children of working mothers has increased recently, receiving endorsements of elected officials and political candidates. The Day Care and Child Development Council, formed in 1968, is now promoting programs of child care service for "children of all ages from conception through youth, to families from every kind of economic and social background and to every community, with priority to those whose need is greatest." Substantial support for programs of day-care is clearly necessary in the case of children of low-income mothers who want to work or undergo job training. If changes are made in arrangements for welfare payments, requiring mothers of dependent children to be employed or in training, the creation of day-care centers will be mandatory.

LIFE EXPECTANCY AND WORKLIFE EXPECTANCY

Repeated references in the literature on labor-force activity of women to the age factor testify to the fact that the stage of a

[4] From a manuscript for a forthcoming volume on research on aging by Matilda A. Riley *et al*.

woman's life-cycle is an important explanatory factor. Hazel Kyrk emphasized this point earlier:

... Working women are not a special and peculiar part of the female population. Rather, they are women at a particular stage of their life span, or those who at the time the count of the labor force was made were experiencing some special exigency or circumstance. The proper question is not, Which women work, but When do women work?[5]

Information on when women work can be drawn from the tables of working life for women. Based on 1960 Census data, these tables show the length of worklife for women of various ages and differing child responsibilities, and under different marital circumstances.[6] Table 5.1 demonstrates that women have an extended working span after they no longer have young children. For example, a thirty-five-year-old woman is usually past the stage of

Table 5.1. Average number of years of labor force activity remaining for selected groups of women in the labor force, 1960

Age	Single women	Married, husband present, no children	Married, husband present, in labor force after birth of last child	Widowed	Divorced
20	45.3	34.9	a	41.8	43.3
25	40.5	30.1	a	37.0	38.5
30	35.7	26.6	a	32.1	33.6
35	31.2	24.4	23.8	27.3	28.8
40	26.3	20.8	19.1	22.5	24.1
45	21.6	16.7	14.5	17.8	19.7
50	17.1	13.7	11.9	13.4	15.5
55	13.1	10.9	9.4	9.8	11.6
60	10.0	8.7	6.9	7.1	8.4
65	7.8	6.5	5.9	6.0	6.7

a Amounts not significant.
SOURCE: Stuart Garfinkle, "Worklife Expectancy and Training Needs for Women," Manpower Report No. 12, May 1967, p. 4.

[5] Hazel Kyrk, *Who Works*, p. 51.
[6] See Table A in Stuart Garfinkle, "Worklife Expectancy," pp. 7–8.

having pre-school children, and may turn her attention to a paying job. Married women in this category have an average remaining worklife expectancy of about twenty-four years.

Marital status, as well as number of children, is an important factor in the worklife picture for women. Single women are likely to have a continuous worklife somewhat comparable to that of men. Widowed and divorced women are similarly inclined to continue in the labor force, and even childless married women have a long worklife. The latter is somewhat shorter, however, because of the availability of the husband's income. A girl of eighteen who is beginning her first job will probably marry and have children; but the older she gets, the less likely she is to marry. Thus single girls of eighteen have an average worklife expectancy of only twenty-five years, whereas single women of twenty-four can expect to work thirty-four years.[7] At present, women tend to retire from the labor force at a younger age than men.

The ability to control family size will be reflected in fewer births and this in turn will increase the worklife expectancy of women. As Garfinkle has noted, the decline in births since 1958 is of some significance. He cites estimates that the birth of a child reduces a married woman's worklife span by about ten years; each additional child lowers worklife by another two or three years. Societal concern with limiting population growth, in combination with improved birth control and legalized abortions,[8] will surely reduce or even eliminate the average length of time women are out of the work force, in the years ahead. Depending on how men and women want their work and leisure (or nonmarket work) apportioned through the life cycle, the worklife of women may come to approximate that of men, with both sexes enjoying either a worklife now shorter than the male's, or a workyear that is shortened by additional vacation time or fewer working hours per week. Family patterns of work, nonmarket work, and leisure activi-

[7] *Ibid.*, p. 4.

[8] At present, thirty-one states allow abortions only when necessary to preserve the mother's life. Nineteen states and the District of Columbia permit additional grounds. In three of these latter states (Alaska, Hawaii, and New York), the decision is up to the woman and her physician.

ties will continue to shift, as both husband and wife pursue careers throughout adult life.

When there is a break in woman's worklife (usually occasioned by the birth of children) the importance of this discontinuity should not be minimized. For one thing, the interruption of market work prevents the woman from building an orderly career in the same way a man does; yet when they return to work, women have to compete for jobs on the same basis as men. It is sometimes possible for a woman to "keep up with her career" by reading and part-time study during her child-bearing period, but this can hardly be equated with job experience. One effect is to discourage ambition.

A second set of problems has to do with the quality of a woman's education and training. Since she thinks that her initial stint in the labor force will probably be a short one, followed by perhaps a decade of home work, she is not likely to make long-run career plans.[9] Nor has she generally been counseled to do so. Both she and her advisers have looked toward her immediate jobs and earnings, frequently motivated by the need for her to support a husband through his continued study. Making a similar investment in her own advanced education could be justified only if she expected to continue working, which is usually not the case.

The fact that most of her worklife occurs after she has had children and reared them to school age is not readily apparent when she is finishing high school or college. But maximizing earnings is clearly important, since she is likely to be paying for a home, furnishings, husband's education, etc. When she is ready to return to a job the skills that were acquired in the previous work experience are no longer up to date. At this stage of her life, what are her chances of acquiring additional education or training?

---

[9] Nor does she pay any particular attention to preparation for her tasks in the home. Morton Hunt notes that although training for homemaking might be justified, it rarely occurs within the formal educational framework, perhaps because of its lack of appeal. "Unfortunately, compared to music and novels, hairdos and clothes, poetry and psychology, dates and dances, housekeeping is dull and unreal; like old age and death, it is inevitable —but not worth worrying about yet." *Her Infinite Variety* (New York: Harper and Row, 1962), p. 154.

With the exception of the guidance offered through the continuing education programs that have appeared during the past two decades, women have had to return to the labor market with little assistance from the educational world. Nor has the concern with job training during the past decade been extended to the particular needs of middle-aged women. Neither the government nor private industry has shown an interest in refurbishing the work skills of the woman of thirty-five; other manpower surpluses (particularly those of youth) have occupied the nation's attention. To a great many people, moreover, it would probably be difficult to defend the expenditure of public funds to train women for market jobs, when they appear to have both husbands to support them, and children who need them at home.

Programs of continuing education, which came to national prominence with the establishment of the one at the University of Minnesota in 1960, attempt to meet some of the educational and job-training needs of women beyond college age. Following the 1957 report of the National Manpower Council (and the 1955 report of the Committee on the Education of Women of The American Council on Education), interest in these programs spread to many American universities and centers were established with both private and public funds. In her statement of the rationale for this movement, Esther Westervelt points to the nation's discovery that women's lives had changed markedly; quite suddenly, the traditional demands on her time had disappeared. Her children were in school, her home required little care, and her husband was away from home most of his working hours. Neighborhood roles, too, were becoming professionalized and woman "was no longer needed to tend the sick, comfort the dying, share her goods with the needy, and help to educate the young. In short, at the prime of her physical powers with more than half of her adult life ahead of her, she found herself without a job."[10]

[10] Esther M. Westervelt, "Education, Vocation, and Avocation in Women's Lives," in Anne F. Scott, *What is Happening to American Women.* (Atlanta: Southern Newspaper Publishing Association Foundation, 1970), pp. 62–63.

By 1970 almost 400 continuing education programs had been established for counseling, referring women to educational or occupational channels, or to job training. Although these programs are attached to educational institutions, they are not usually well integrated with the universities' curricular structure. Nor do they have the appearance of long-term commitments, with financial arrangements that will allow for stability and growth. The low priority attached to such endeavors will remain low as long as educational institutions continue to face the budgetary crises now widespread. In the face of much more dramatic demands for an extension of higher education to all youth, pleas for the allocation of scarce funds to the education of middle-aged women will probably draw little new support. Some of the programs now under way are being carried by the momentum provided in a less stringent financial period.

The appearance of "women's studies" programs is now receiving much the same attention that continuing education merited a decade or so ago. According to one report, about fifty-five colleges and universities were offering at least one course in this new area at the beginning of 1971. In a few instances a new field of study similar to black studies is being planned, with a research component as well as a series of courses. The significance of this latest move is difficult to predict: the extent to which the courses will be taken by men as well as women, the relationship of the courses to social and natural sciences, and even the objectives of studies of this sort are not yet clear. The enthusiasm of undergraduate women for courses of this nature is impressive, however. In contrast to the marginal support given to continuing education programs, "women's studies" courses are rapidly being written into college curricula. And although research has not been a major component of these studies to date, the courses may well develop a greater interest in the work problems facing women, and eventually lead to research on the questions so frequently raised.

6

The Future:
Some Things We Don't Know about Women

Equality for women is now a popular cause whose history of achievement is marked by slow and sometimes grudging assent.[1] Journalist Jurate Kazickas, taking account of the recent opening of a famous bar to women customers, noted that "It took women 70 years to get the vote, almost half a century to get an Equal

[1] For a discussion of the extent of discriminatory practices in employment in other countries, see "Discrimination in Employment or Occupation on the Basis of Marital Status," I, *International Labor Review*, vol. 85 (March, 1962), pp. 263–82; and II, (April, 1962), pp. 368–89. The current status of women in the labor force in major European countries is reviewed in *Participation of Women in the Economic and Social Development of Their Countries*, United Nations Commission on the Status of Women (New York; United Nations Publications, 1970). About one-third of the sixty nations participating in the survey concerning discrimination on the basis of marital status replied that there were no discriminatory practices on the basis of sex, in particular marital status, in public or private employment. In the sixty countries there is not often anything in the general legislation prohibiting or restricting the employment of married women; but there are also very few constitutions which contain an express provision prohibiting employment discrimination on the basis of marital status. Marital status thus could be the basis of discriminatory practices in many of the countries (two-thirds of those questioned). In the absence of provisions specifically stipulating that there shall be no discrimination on the ground of sex and marital status, such practices may come into being or persist in certain countries or in certain industries.

Rights Amendment approved in the House, two hundred years to receive college educations, and 116 years to get into New York's McSorley's bar."

The Equal Rights Amendment which was introduced and passed by the House in the summer of 1970 but eventually lost in the Senate, would have provided that "equality of rights under the law shall not be denied or abridged by the United States or by any State on account of sex."

THE ISSUE OF SEX DISCRIMINATION IN EMPLOYMENT

During the discussions of the amendment, Congresswoman Martha Griffiths, one of its sponsors, spoke of her fear "that we are heading into a repressive society and the only group left to op-

---

In an effort to overcome prejudice against the employment of women, irrespective of marital status, many governments have pursued both corrective legal measures and educational campaigns. In recent years the status of women in major European countries seems to have improved and by some measures has surpassed the level in this country. In 1968, European women's average wages as a proportion of wages paid to men ranged from slightly under 60 percent in Britain, to 70 percent in West Germany, 74 percent in Italy, and 86 percent in France. In all the above countries, the wage gap has narrowed since 1955. In contrast, the average wage of women in the U.S. is only 58 percent of the median male paycheck, and the gap between male and female wages has widened since 1955. European women are now less concentrated in clerical work, and areas traditionally relegated to members of the female sex in this country.

Women's improvements in relative wage rate and participation in traditionally male-dominated roles may be partially attributed to a tight labor market. They may also reflect the impact of rapid political, technological, economic, and social developments. The extent of discrimination has lessened in those countries where social progress has been rapid, according to The United Nations Commission on the Status of Women; nevertheless, in a majority of countries, both developed and developing, the women's role is still quite limited. In most countries, whatever their stage of development, obstacles to equity for women in the labor force are apparent: lack of proper education and training; lack of vocational guidance and counselling; traditional attitudes of both men and women towards their respective roles in society; the division of the labor market into traditionally "male" and "female" sectors; lack of child-care facilities of working mothers; and lack of labor-saving devices in the home. For an analysis of women in developing nations see Ester Boserup, *Woman's Role in Economic Development* (New York: St. Martin's Press, 1970).

press is women." Along with many other supporters of the measure (including several Commissions on the Status of Women), Congressmen argued that Supreme Court decisions under the Fifth and the Fourteenth Amendments denied women equal treatment under the law; hence women's need for a clear constitutional guarantee against discriminatory legislation.

Opponents of the amendment replied that women were assured legal equality under the due process clause of the Fifth Amendment and the equal protection clause of the Fourteenth, as well as certain legislation such as the U. S. Equal Pay Act of 1963 and Title VII of the Civil Rights Act of 1964. The new amendment was "too generally worded, applied to too wide a range of activities and concerned too sensitive a social issue to produce instant equality."[2] Moreover, they cited the cases of protective labor legislation applying only to women as one of the serious losses such an amendment would bring.

Among supporters and many of the opponents of the Equal Rights Amendment, there was agreement that sex discrimination does exist, and that it is particularly damaging to women on the job or seeking a job. The Presidential Task Force on Women's Rights and Responsibilities concluded that discriminatory practices against women are so widespread and pervasive that they have often come to be regarded as normal. As earlier discussion noted, the Equal Employment Opportunity Commission has found that about one-third of the charges made under Title VII of the Civil Rights Act are cases of alleged discrimination on the basis of sex. In the last fiscal year 3,597 such complaints fell within the Commission's jurisdiction. Further documentation comes from the Labor Department, which has found that under the terms of the Equal Pay Act about 54,000 employees, mostly women, have been underpaid $18.7 million since 1963. More than 170 lawsuits have been filed to recover the back pay.[3]

[2] For a summary of the arguments for and against the amendment, see *AAUW Journal* (October, 1970), pp. 3 and 11.

[3] Jim Hyatt, "Women at Work," *Wall Street Journal* (September 21, 1970), pp. 1, 8.

In the face of such practices it is understandable that women workers are angry, that organizations pushing for women's rights are working overtime, and that the press is having a field day. Proponents of women's causes find that one of the major problems is to persuade the public that sex discrimination is a serious matter, similar in many respects to racial discrimination. "It's a scandalous situation," the founder of Women's Equity Action League (WEAL) complained, "and then everybody tries to pretend that women who feel the way I do are a bunch of male-hating freaks."[4]

Although there seems to be broad support for equal rights for women, many questions are raised regarding the possible losses they may suffer in the bargain. Protective labor legislation regulating the number of hours a woman may work, the weight she may lift, etc., was designed to prevent exploitation of females. As late as the 1950's it was argued that working women, more than any other group, remained incapable of protecting themselves. "In industry, women are more likely than men to work for marginal businesses characterized by small size, low capital investment, low profit margins, haphazard personnel practices, high employee turnover and low pay."[5]

The concept of the woman as a marginal worker persists, not only because of the kind of work she does, but also because she is often the family's second worker, whose earnings are not considered essential to the family's welfare. In the past, employers were often inclined to lay off married women first, in times of personnel cutbacks; even today, the practice of giving preference in hiring to men "who have families to support" is not unknown. In addition to sex discrimination that is excused on the basis of a concern for the most needy job seekers, employers have cited other reasons for their failure to hire women: they have higher absentee rates and are in and out of the labor force more frequently than men; their productivity rates are lower than men's; it costs more to employ women because of state regulations requiring special rest-

[4] *Ibid.*, p. 1.
[5] Robert W. Smuts, *Women and Work in America* (New York: Columbia University Press, 1959), p. 105.

93

room facilities. To most of these objections, substantiating evidence is lacking.[6] Still, progress toward equality of treatment in hiring, particularly, has been slow.

The Federal Civil Rights Act[7]

Title VII of the Civil Rights Act of 1964 prohibits sex discrimination in private employment, as well as discriminatory practices based on race, color, religion, and national origin. Administered by the Equal Employment Opportunity Commission, the title generally covers employers with twenty-five or more employees and specifies that it is unlawful

for employers to fail or refuse to hire, to discharge, or otherwise to discriminate against a person with respect to compensation, terms, conditions, or privileges of employment on the basis of sex; to limit, segregate, or classify employees in such a way as to deprive any individual of employment opportunities or otherwise adversely affect the employee's status, on the basis of sex. . . .

Labor organizations may not exclude women from membership, or limit, classify, or segregate members on the basis of sex. Employment agencies may not fail or refuse to refer for employment, or otherwise discriminate; nor may employers, labor organizations, or employment agencies indicate preference, limitation, or specification based on sex. Finally, none of the three groups may discriminate with respect to training or retraining programs.

Exceptions to these general rules may be allowed if "sex is a bona fide occupational qualification,"[8] or if differentials are based

[6] For a reference to several studies of sex differences in work performance, absenteeism, and labor turnover, see Esther Peterson, "Working Women," *Daedalus* (Spring, 1964), pp. 671–99.

[7] This discussion of federal and state laws pertaining to sex discrimination relies heavily on U.S. Department of Labor, *Laws on Sex Discrimination in Employment* (1970).

[8] The guidelines indicate that the Commission will find that the following situations do not qualify as bona fide occupational exceptions:
1. Refusal to hire a woman because of assumptions as to comparative characteristics of women in general. Example: the assumption that the turnover rate is higher among women.

on ability tests not intended to discriminate. The title does not rule out the payment of differentials in different locations or those based on seniority, merit, or incentive system. Examples of violations of these rules have been cited: refusal to have a woman as account executive in an advertising firm on the basis that clients would not accept a woman; denial of promotion of a woman to a management post because males in the company would not work with a woman; denial of a job as electronics assembler to a man because women are better at this work.[9]

State Fair Employment Practices Laws

As of early 1970, thirty-seven states, the District of Columbia and Puerto Rico have mandatory fair employment practices laws; twenty-one of these states and the District of Columbia prohibit sex discrimination. Of the latter group, most were passed in the last half of the nineteen-sixties, their coverage differing somewhat from the Federal law: some states cover all employers and several cover only those having twenty-five or more employees; some states include public as well as private employment; two states extend only to employers, the others specifying labor organizations and employment agencies as well. Domestic service employees and family employment are exempt in many of the states, although not exempt under the Civil Rights Act.

State laws tend to prohibit the same employment practices outlawed by the Civil Rights Act, with some differences in wording.

---

2. Refusal to hire because of stereotyped characterizations of the sexes. Examples: men are less capable of assembling intricate equipment; women are less capable of aggressive salesmanship.
3. Refusal to hire because of preferences of co-workers, the employer, clients or customers.
4. The need to provide separate facilities, except where expense would be unreasonable.

A bona fide exception occurs, however, when it is necessary for authenticity or genuineness, as in the case of an actor or actress.

[9] See *Sex Discrimination in Employment Practices*, Report on a conference held at University of California at Los Angeles (Washington: U.S. Department of Labor, 1970), pp. 12–13.

Four states do not prohibit discriminatory advertising; only about half the states include references to training programs. Exceptions, too, roughly parallel those of the Federal law in most of the states; sex as a bona fide occupational qualification is recognized in all state laws except three. The major provisions of the Civil Rights Act and the state laws, as they relate to sex discrimination in employment, have been summarized in *Laws on Sex Discrimination and Employment*, released by the U. S. Department of Labor in 1970.

Conflicts between State and Federal fair employment practices statutes and state protective legislation

State laws providing protection for women workers—regulations of the hours they may work, the lifting of weights in excess of certain limits, their employment in some jobs—have been held in conflict with the anti-discrimination provisions of the Civil Rights Act and state laws which specify that employers may not treat women differently in hiring and other conditions of employment.

When the issue has been that of the contradictory provisions of state laws, different opinions have resulted. Several state fair employment practice laws specify that their provisions do not void protective labor laws; others permit differentiation on the basis of sex, if state laws require. But the attorney general of Pennsylvania has ruled that the Women's Labor Law of 1913, which required work breaks, seating at work, rest and dressing rooms, etc., thus giving preferential treatment to women, was no longer necessary.

Recent social and economic changes have improved the status of females so that they now enjoy a status substantially equal to that of males in all areas of employment opportunities. Thus, the conditions prompting the enactment of the 1913 statute no longer exist. As a matter of fact, females now enjoy the freedom to be employed under conditions and hours of employment equivalent to that of males. . . .[10]

[10] *Laws on Sex Discrimination in Employment*, p. 9.

96

In the case of conflicts between state protective laws and the Civil Rights Act, the argument was advanced that Congress intended only to provide equal opportunity for women, not to negate their need for protection. But the counter claim that the state laws were inherently discriminatory has been made repeatedly. Several states have concluded that their laws limiting the hours of women's work must yield to Title VII, and a few have stated that they would continue to enforce the hours regulation until a federal court rules otherwise. The Equal Employment Opportunity Commission issued new guidelines in August, 1969, which paralleled the Pennsylvania opinion:

. . . Such State laws and regulations, although originally promulgated for the purpose of protecting females, have ceased to be relevant to our technology or to the expanding role of the female worker in our economy. The Commission has found that such laws do not take into account the capacities, preferences, and abilities of individual females and tend to discriminate rather than protect. Accordingly, the Commission has concluded that such laws and regulations conflict with Title VII of the Civil Rights Act of 1964 and will not be considered a defense to an otherwise established unlawful employment practice or as a basis for the application of the bona fide occupational qualification exception.[11]

Although several cases involving sex discrimination have reached the courts, none have gone to the Supreme Court. The weightlifting restriction has frequently been the basis for failing to hire women; none of the courts have agreed that employers may bar women from jobs on this basis. One case, involving both the lifting of weights and the working of overtime, is expected to go to the Supreme Court for resolution of the issue of state protective legislation versus the nondiscriminatory provision of Title VII.

Other sex differences under the law

The primary thrust of recent anti-discrimination measures is directed toward conditions of employment. But other important questions were involved in the Equal Rights Amendment, and to

[11] *Ibid.*, p. 10.

some women the threats in the Amendment were greater than its promises. Drafting of women for military service, on a basis comparable to that for men; awarding of child custody to either parent in a divorce case, the support for children possibly becoming the legal obligation of the mother as well as the father; insistence that women serve the same public obligations, such as jury duty, as men—these, plus the removal of protective legislation, called attention to the extremely wide differences in treatment of the two sexes under federal and state law. The basic question of whether such differences have been in the public interest, and especially in women's best interest, can no longer be avoided.

In our history we have not an instance in which a significant number of women have challenged the legal status of women, the manner of determining economic rewards afforded them in their jobs, and even the traditional division of responsibility between the sexes. Such a challenge is now here. So what is viewed as a demand for removal of sex discrimination in the workplace is a bit more: it is a demand for much wider lifestyle options for women. By implication, men's roles, too, both in the home and in the job market, can be expected to undergo some change.

THE SLOW PROCESS OF CHANGING THE RULES

If the campaign which many women are now waging on behalf of their right to work throughout life, as men do; to receive equal pay for equal work; to be hired on the basis of credentials rather than sex—if these efforts have the effect of rewriting labor legislation and changing employment practices, there will inevitably be a new look in the sexual division of labor. Both men and women will come to have a wider range of occupations. The change is likely to be a gradual one, however. The number of women willing to forego marriage and family, or shift child-rearing responsibilities to men or day-care centers cannot be predicted with any accuracy, but changes in attitude toward "women's place" seem to require a basic departure from present thinking. Historian Carl Degler has warned us against chalking up too much progress in women's employment conditions during the decades following the Second World War:

Measured in the number of women working, the changes in the economic position of women add up to a feminist success. . . . But weighed in the scales of quality instead of quantity, the changes in women's economic status are not so striking. It is true that women now work in virtually every job listed by the Bureau of the Census. . . . Yet the fact remains that the occupations in which the vast majority of women actually engage are remarkably similar to those historically held by women.[12]

A change in attitude as to which jobs are appropriate for women and which for men is only half the battle. Women who would move into higher-level jobs will be expected to observe the rules by which such persons are educated—rules which may be incompatible with the woman's self-concept. If Morton Hunt's incisive comments on "the cool mood and the split career"[13] approach which women displayed in the past decade are applicable to the 1970's, the supply of female talent may fall short of the demand. In fact, employers have been protesting the charge of sex discrimination, claiming instead that women are either untrained for top jobs, or unwilling to give these jobs their complete dedication.

Until recently, there was ample evidence of a decline in the proportion of women willing to undergo the extensive education necessary to qualify for some professions; however, even when women did qualify for these professions, their rewards did not match those of men in similar circumstances.[14] Some women's aspirations and their dedication to work may improve, along with their job horizons, and as a result the small proportion of women scaling business and professional heights may rise. But how much improvement will there be in, say, the decade of the seventies? How close will we come to achieving the goal Alice Rossi set forth in her "Equality Between Sexes: An Immodest Proposal"?[15]

[12] Carl N. Degler, "The Changing Place of Women in America," *Daedalus* (Spring, 1964), p. 661.

[13] Morton Hunt, *Her Infinite Variety,* p. 268.

[14] See chapter 3.

[15] *Daedalus,* vol. 93 (Spring, 1964), pp. 607–52.

Despite Professor Rossi's persuasive reasoning, both men and women seem to harbor a good bit of opposition to such equality. On the male view, first:

no doubt there exists among men an honest sense of wishing to save at whatever cost a sexual polarity, a vital tension and an essential difference which they fear may be lost in too much sameness, equality, and equivalance, or at any rate in too much self-conscious talk.[16]

This same fear of sameness may plague women, but the more common explanation for anxiety in women turns on the tendency to equate achievement with loss of feminity; hence "in achievement-oriented situations, women will worry not only about failure, but about success."[17] One recent study found that a woman's wish to achieve conflicts with her wish to avoid success, for "If she fails, she is not living up to her own standards of performance; if she succeeds, she is not living up to societal expectations about the female role."[18]

Many other writers have criticized women's seeming lack of professional ambition—criticism which under close examination, usually emerges as praise. The preoccupation of the female with love and marriage is fully accepted. It is only when she displays "the old-style careerist's scorching ambition and hostility toward men"[19] that she has to explain herself. Currently, many men and women resist taking women's new career interests seriously. No dinner party is now complete without a few derisive comments on women's ambitions to be stevedores or lumberjacks. Members of both sexes are apprehensive, men perhaps more than women: "Where dominant identities depend on being dominant, it is hard to grant equality to the dominated."[20]

[16] Erik H. Erikson, "Inner and Outer Space: Reflections on Womanhood," *Daedalus*, vol. 93 (Spring, 1964), p. 584.

[17] Joy D. Osofsky, "The Socialization and Education of American Women," in Scott, *What Is Happening*, p. 37.

[18] Matina Horner, "Women's Motive to Avoid Success," *Psychology Today*, vol. 62 (November, 1969), pp. 36–38.

[19] Morton Hunt, *Her Infinite Variety*, p. 262.

[20] Erik H. Erikson, "Inner and Outer Space." "And finally, where one feels exposed, threatened, or cornered, it is difficult to be judicious," p. 585.

Having so many women at work but so few women in law, medicine, and the sciences has been attributed to the absence of any feminist ideology. Writing early in the 1960's, Carl Degler maintained that in this country there is not now and never has been an ideological basis for the movement of women into the labor force. With American women, as with American society, interest in the job is an immediate and practical one; it is jobs, not careers, that women have sought. "To say . . . that men have opposed and resisted the opening of opportunities to women is to utter only a half truth. The whole truth is that American society in general, which includes women, shuns like a disease any feminist ideology."[21] Although he clearly applauds Professor Rossi's proposal for equality of the sexes, he concludes that most American women still do not want outside work justified as a normal pattern for married women; they prefer instead to think of such work as special. And as long as women view their work in this way "the soil is thin and the climate incongenial for the growth of any seedlings of ideology."[22]

THE QUESTION OF LIBERATION

Degler's astute appraisal of the limited work interests of most American women in the past must now be cast in the perspective of the new thrust for women's rights. Is something different in the making? And will enough women join to qualify this wave of interest as a woman's movement, even an ideology? Finally, is such a movement an effective tool of change? Answers to these questions lie outside the economists' competence, true. Yet one can say very little about the future labor force activity of women except by reference to the more pervasive issues affecting women's work preferences.

It is well to remember how far we have come along the path toward sex equality in the labor force, along with how far we

[21] Degler, "The Changing Place," p. 663.
[22] *Ibid.*, p. 670.

have yet to go. It was in September, 1957, that a New York City
newspaper reporter asked four people at random: "What would
happen if all working wives gave up their jobs tomorrow?" A secretary said children would get more attention, resulting in less
delinquency; in any event, husbands earned enough to support
their families. A singer, also female, said that the effect would be
to give better jobs to working girls who really needed them, since
"the majority of married women who go to business do so to earn
money for luxuries like mink stoles. . . ." A man from Brooklyn
thought that in time it would mean higher wages for men. A male
post office employee said it would result in a better home life for
husband, wife, and family.[23]

At that time, a similar poll in any American city would probably have yielded similar results. But public endorsement of wom-
en's campaigns in the 1970's would seem to indicate a change in
attitude. Large numbers of women have joined the protest marches
under the banner of liberation for women, and it is significant
that these are increasingly the young women, many of them still
in school. Their impact on working women a few years from now
will surely be an important one. Admittedly, these younger women
may be somewhat naive in their perception of the opposition they
will face from some quarters. Commenting on the attitudes revealed in the earlier comments, Erwin Canham noted the problems
ahead: "Look at the misconceptions; look at the jealousy toward
married women on the part of the interviewed females . . .; the
jealousy, possessiveness, and prejudice on the part of men."[24]

Misconceptions may serve to deter women from taking more
active roles—misconceptions, in particular, as to what men prefer
women to be. Data collected from over 20,000 men and women
in several countries—England, France, Germany, Czechoslovakia,
Greece, Turkey, Iran, the Philippines, Japan, countries of South
America, and the United States—by the Maferr Foundation (Male

[23] From Esther Lloyd-Jones, "Education for Reentry into the Labor
Force," in National Manpower Council, *Work in the Lives of Married
Women* (New York: Columbia University Press, 1958), pp. 27–40.
[24] "Womanpower in Today's World," p. 14.

and Female Role Research) reveal some interesting perceptions of the female role. These questions were posed: How do women view themselves, both as they are and would like to be, and as they think men would like them to be? And what do men see as the ideal woman?

Reporting on the sample of 1,200 American women and 600 American men, Anne Steinmann finds that women revealed a great discrepancy between what they viewed as the ideal feminine role and what they thought men wanted them to be. Women accepted some parts of the passive role, but also had aspirations and ambitions of their own. Their perception of what men wanted in women was quite different, however; men looked, women thought, for the "strongly passive, family-oriented woman who refrained from seeking outside achieving activity."[25] In reality, men's concept of the ideal woman was not the one imputed to them. They preferred elements of both passivity and activity, or in general the ideal to which the women in the sample said they aspired.

The author poses the question of whether women's ascribing to men a set of standards for women which men in fact do not hold arises from inner conflict or ambivalence on the part of the woman. Does the woman, feeling the pressure to achieve on her own yet longing also to be somewhat dependent, project onto the man her rejected expectation of a dependent female? Expressing a concern for conflicts which may arise from women's need for and denial of dependency, the psychologist concludes that "the goal for women's liberation should not only be one of helping the American woman to achieve her right to personal achievement, but also to accept the dualism within herself and her right to . . . aggressive and passive tendencies."[26]

Indeed, there may be some tendency to overestimate the extent to which men long for wives who do not work outside their homes; the rapid rise in labor force activity of married women would indicate a widespread male willingness, at least, to endorse the prac-

[25] Anne Steinmann, "The Ambivalent Woman," *New Generation*, vol. 51 (Fall, 1969), p. 30.
[26] *Ibid.*, p. 32.

tice. But the questions are now more complex than that of a wife's working or not working. The issues have to do with certain marketplace considerations: the kinds of work available to women, the pay and professional advancement that accompany different jobs, equality of treatment in all aspects of work; and the equally important matters related to the domestic division of labor: whose career takes precedence in job changes, whether the wife assumes complete responsibility for child care, how much investment the family makes in the education of the female as compared with that of the male.

On the domestic scene, resolution of the current questions has important implications for family living patterns. Along with the restriction in family size, the emphasis on women's right to participate freely in market activities will surely lead the married couple to consider the wife's job more important than heretofore and to plan around her career as well as the husband's. More women, too, may remain unmarried, or seek divorces; careers will inevitably absorb the interests of many competent women who no longer need the financial support of a husband and who are not particularly interested in having children. Wider social acceptance of the unmarried female is already apparent, and contraceptive methods now make it unnecessary for the single woman to forego sexual relationships.

In the marketplace, whatever progress women make will probably be made piece-meal by arguing each specific issue in the courts and at the bargaining table. It is noteworthy that women's emphasis on improved working conditions has paid little attention to the possible advantages of union organization; justice is to be more legislated than bargained, apparently. But some of the new demands can be achieved only through negotiation, and maintained in the way men have maintained their position in the work force, i.e., through day-to-day surveillance. What women have to acknowledge, eventually, is that rhetoric is no substitute for bargaining strength.

The strength women have gained from the liberation movement is difficult to assess at this early stage. If the failure to gain passage of the Equal Rights Amendment is the test, the movement's political position is a weak one. But the widespread interest in women's rights that surrounded that debate, and the present sensitivity of employers to antidiscriminatory legislation surely attest to the effectiveness of women's activism on their own behalf.

The militant stance of some of the women's liberationists is surely repugnant to many persons of both sexes who are nevertheless strong supporters of improved working conditions for women. There is some reluctance on the part of both working women and housewives to espouse a cause they view as hostile to the men they are closest to—employers, husbands, and fathers. Ideological differences between members of a family are not unknown, of course; basically different views are frequently held by middle-aged parents and their college-age children, for example, and between the former and their own elderly parents. It is interesting to note that in intergenerational conflicts there is nevertheless a dominant group—those at middle age—who make most of the major decisions and in large measure control the lives of the others. Of further interest is the increasing degree of conflict between the middle-aged and youth over the decision-making power.

Women who have no interest in working outside the home— well over half the total number—are less likely than working women to be interested in their sisters' treatment in the marketplace; moreover, we have no data on the proportion of women who think of other women as their "sisters" in the manner suggested by the liberation literature. Analogies between Negroes' fight for equal rights and that of women have frequently been drawn, but comparison of the two cases reveals as many differences as similarities. Women, like Negroes, have had the poorer paying jobs, have been expected to assume a certain role, and have been denied access to particular areas of activity. But the class and income a woman achieves is dependent primarily on the success of her father or husband, and she has every reason to promote his cause, often even when it conflicts with her own career interests. No such commonality exists between whites and blacks.

It has been argued that women constitute the one case in which servants marry their masters. If the delineation is correct, one is obliged to point out that marriage may not altogether wipe the master-servant distinction from the minds of either sex; still, intermarriage does weaken the basis for any concerted action of one group against the other. Ardent spokesmen for a women's movement recognize the difficulty of uniting women in the cause of freeing themselves from oppression, given the proximity, always, of the oppressor. Nevertheless, they argue, "We are a class, we are oppressed as a class . . . . Purposely divided from each other, each of us is ruled by one or more men for the benefit of all men." The acceptance of a common identity is necessary, because "there is no personal escape, no personal salvation, no personal solution."[27]

When the female liberation movement comes to focus on women's jobs, salaries, and working conditions in the marketplace (as opposed to the views on household chores, against which the movement has launched even stronger protests), the major demand has been mainly for legal protection against sex discrimination, for day care centers to free mothers to work, and for an upgrading of job levels. The mechanisms for accomplishing the last goal have not been adequately explored, however. What steps do women take to avoid clerical jobs and enter instead the professions? How can they bring about higher levels of pay for those jobs that for a while, at least, are likely to be dominated by women?

Unfortunately, discussions of the necessary investments in human capital, reductions in supply of certain types of labor, the need for collective bargaining strength—factors which are most often cited as means of improving the wage position of any group of workers—are not often found in the writings on female liberation. Yet all of these routes must be pursued, along with that of improving women's legal status, if the goals are to be achieved. If women would make economic gains, they need to realize that market forces do have an impact, and that they cannot continue to offer an excess supply of a particular talent such as elementary

[27] Beverly Jones and Judith Brown, "Toward a Female Liberation Movement," in Leslie B. Tanner, ed., *Voices From Women's Liberation* (New York: New American Library, 1970), p. 387.

school teaching, and yet expect the salary for that job to keep pace with that in professions which are understaffed.

One of the most interesting single research questions has to do with the degree of acceptance of the liberation movement among mature women. What proportion of today's women espouse true equality of treatment in the labor market and in the courts? How many women take the cause seriously, to the point of lodging a complaint when necessary, and how many are either intimidated by male employers or actually enjoy being protected and a bit "special" because they work, though women?

The emphasis which female high school and college students are currently giving to women's rights, job status, and freedom of behavior is highly significant, since these women will soon enter the work force. Again, an intriguing question arises. Is this generation of young women (and young men, for they too argue for women's equality) typical of those to follow? If so, the relationship of the sexes in both the home and the marketplace will hereafter be different. If, instead, the cohort now in high school and college will be followed by a cohort whose social concerns lie elsewhere, or who actually prefer the more traditional family patterns, the effect of current efforts to improve women's lot will dissipate somewhat.

Even so, it seems unlikely that American women, particularly the college-educated, will again give home work and child care the central role they occupied in, say, the 1940's and 1950's. The greater the societal need to restrict family size, moreover, the greater will be women's participation in market jobs. The one significant deterrent to this movement of women into the labor force would be a substantial decline in the demand for those services typically performed by women. But such a decline would have only a shortrun effect, and could easily be offset by opening to women a broader range of job opportunities.

In addition to the question of the extent to which women of all ages and labor force positions subscribe to the current liberation movement, and the question of whether the cohort of women now, say, aged fifteen to twenty-five will be succeeded by cohorts of similar persuasion, the increased labor force activity of women raises interesting questions related to the future allocation of time among the three uses: market work, home work, and leisure. With the growth in productivity per manhour afforded by improved technology, and the increased labor force size afforded by women's entrance to the labor force, a growth in time free of market work should also ensue. Will the change in the sex composition of the labor force have the effect of shortening weekly hours, lengthening annual vacations, or shortening worklife?

Productivity gains in this country have conferred increases in nonworking time during the twentieth century, with the forms of the leisure varying from one period to another. Reductions in weekly hours of work occurred mainly in the first third of the century; increases in vacation, sick leave, etc., followed in the decades of the 1940's and 1950's. In addition to these workyear changes, the age of labor force entry for males rose significantly and their age of retirement from work dropped, which, with increased life expectancy, added about nine years of nonworking time to the male's life in the first half of the century.

Throughout this period women's labor force activity grew, albeit unevenly, and one could argue that there has been some tradeoff between the free-time gains of men and the free-time losses of women. To the extent that men take over household and child care responsibilities so that wives may work, however, the result is merely a redivision of market and non-market work between the sexes. But will the fact that both husband and wife have full-time jobs not generate a demand for a reduction in the amount of market work each does? Women have traditionally needed short workweeks in order to meet family responsibilities; increased involvement of men in home work may affect their market work-nonmarket work tradeoff in the same way. Given the higher family incomes that result from wives' earnings, moreover, it seems likely that shortened workweeks (or lengthened vacations) will be of somewhat greater value to workers than still greater incomes. The sex allocation of the adult's time between market work and nonmarket activity may thus undergo important changes which, in turn, could affect patterns of working time in industry.

Selected Bibliography

Abbott, Edith. *Women in Industry*. New York: D. Appleton & Co., 1910.

American Science Manpower. National Science Foundation, NSF 66–29. Washington: U.S. Government Printing Office, 1964.

Anderson, Locke, and Jarvis Babcock. "Measuring Potential Gross National Product." Paper delivered at the Meeting of the Econometric Society, 1964.

Angel, Jurenal Londen. *Careers for Women in the Legal Profession*. New York: New York World Trade Academy Press, 1961.

Angrist, Shirley. "Leisure and the Educated Woman," *AAUW Journal*, 60 (October 1966), pp. 10–12.

Ashenfelter, Orley. "Changes in Labor Market Discrimination Over Time," *The Journal of Human Resources*, 5 (Fall 1970), pp. 403–30.

Astin, Helen. *The Woman Doctorate in America: Origins, Career, and Family*. New York: Russell Sage Foundation, 1969.

Axelson, Leland J. "The Marital Adjustment and Marital Role Definitions of Husbands of Working and Nonworking Wives," *Marriage and Family Living*, 25 (May 1963), pp. 189–95.

Bancroft, Gertrude. *The American Labor Force*. New York: John Wiley and Sons, Inc., 1958.

———. "Labor Force Growth and Job Opportunities: Some Doctrines and the Evidence," *Exploring the Dimensions of the Manpower Revolution*, Vol. I: *Selected Reading in Employment and Man-*

power. U.S. Senate, Committee on Labor and Public Welfare, Subcommittee on Employment and Manpower, 88th Congress, 2nd Session. Washington, 1964.

Bayer, Alan E., and Helen S. Astin. "Sex Differences in Academic Rank and Salary Among Science Doctorates in Teaching," *Journal of Human Resources*, 3 (Spring 1968), pp. 191–200.

Bernard, Jessie. *Academic Women*. University Park: Pennsylvania State University Press, 1964.

Blau, Peter, *et al.* "Occupational Choice: A Conceptual Framework," *Industrial and Labor Relations Review*, 9 (July 1956), pp. 531–43.

Boserup, Ester. *Woman's Role in Economic Development*. New York: St. Martin's Press, 1970.

Bowen, William G., and T. Aldrich Finegan. *The Economics of Labor Force Participation*. Princeton: Princeton University Press, 1969.

Bunting, Mary I. "A Huge Waste: Education Womanpower," *New York Times Magazine*, May 7, 1961, p. 23.

Business in Brief. Chase Manhattan Bank, October 1970.

Cain, Glen. *Married Women in the Labor Force*. Chicago: University of Chicago Press, 1966.

Canham, Erwin D. "Womanpower in Today's World," National Manpower Council, *Work in the Lives of Married Women*. New York: Columbia University Press, 1958.

Careers of Ph.D.'s, Academic v. Nonacademic, A Second Report on Followups of Doctorate Cohorts, 1935–60. Washington: National Academy of Sciences, 1968.

Cavanaugh, Aileen. "Present Opportunities for Women in Professional Engineering," *Women in Professional Engineering*. New York: Society of Women Engineers, 1962.

Chronicle of Higher Education, 5 (November 30, 1970).

Clark, Colin. "The Economics of Housework," *Bulletin of the Oxford Institute of Statistics*, 20 (May 1958).

Cohen, Malcolm S. "Married Women in the Labor Force: An Analysis of Participation Rates," *Monthly Labor Review*, 92 (October 1969), pp. 31–35.

Collier, Virginia MacMakin. *Marriage and Careers: A Study of One Hundred Women Who are Wives, Mothers, Homemakers and Professional Women*. New York: The Channel Bookshop, 1926.

Committee on University Women. *Women in the University of Chicago*. May 1970.

Conference of the University-National Bureau Committee for Economic Research. *Aspects of Labor Economics*. Princeton: Princeton University Press, 1962.

David, Opal D. (ed.). *The Education of Women: Signs for the Future.* Washington: American Council on Education, 1959.

Degler, Carl N. "The Changing Place of Women in America," *Daedalus,* 93 (Spring 1964), pp. 653–70.

Diamond, M. C. "Women in Modern Science," *Journal of the American Medical Women's Association,* 18 (November 1963), pp. 891–96.

"Discrimination in Employment or Occupation on the Basis of Marital Status: I," *International Labour Review,* 85 (March 1962), pp. 262–82.

"Discrimination in Employment or Occupation on the Basis of Marital Status: II," *International Labour Review,* 85 (April 1962), pp. 368–69.

Dodge, Norton T. *Women in the Soviet Economy.* Baltimore: Johns Hopkins Press. 1966.

Douglas, Paul H., and Erika H. Schoenberg. "Studies in the Supply Curve of Labor," *Journal of Political Economy,* 45 (February 1937), pp. 45–79.

Dunham, Ralph E., Patricia D. Wright, and Marjorie O. Chandler. *Higher Colleges.* U.S. Office of Education. Washington: U.S. Government Printing Office, 1966.

————. "Teaching Faculty in Universities and Four-Year Colleges." U. S. Office of Education. Washington: U. S. Government Printing Office, 1966.

Endicott, Frank S. "Trends in Employment of College and University Graduates in Business and Industry." Northwestern University, 1970.

Epstein, Cynthia Fuchs. "Women and Professional Careers: The Case of the Woman Lawyer." Unpublished Ph.D. dissertation, Columbia University, 1968.

————. *Woman's Place.* Berkeley: University of California Press, 1970.

Erikson, Erik H. "Inner and Outer Space: Reflections on Womanhood," *Daedalus,* 93 (Spring 1964), pp. 582–606.

Farber, Seymour M., and Roger H. L. Wilson (eds.). *The Potential of Women.* New York: McGraw-Hill, 1963.

Finegan, Aldrich T. "Hours of Work in the United States: A Cross Sectional Analysis," *Journal of Political Economy,* 70 (1962).

Gage, Marie G. "The Work Load and Its Value for 50 Homemakers, Tompkins County, New York." Unpublished Ph.D. dissertation, Cornell University, 1960.

Garfinkle, Stuart H. "Worklife Expectancy and Training Needs of

Women." U. S. Department of Labor, Manpower Report No. 12, May 1967.

Gelber, Sylva. "The Labour Force; the GNP; and Unpaid Housekeeping Services." Ottawa: Canadian Department of Labour, June 1970.

Ghiselli, E. E., M. Haire, and L. W. Porter. "Psychological Research on Pay: An Overview," *Industrial Relations*, 3 (1963), pp. 3–4.

Ginder, Charles. "The Factor of Sex in Office Employment," *Office Executive*, February 1961, p. 10.

Ginzberg, Eli. *Occupational Choice.* New York: Columbia University Press, 1951.

———. *Life Styles of Educated Women.* New York: Columbia University Press, 1966.

Graham, Patricia Albjerg. "Women in Academe," *Science*, 169 (September 25, 1970), pp. 1284–90.

De Grazia, Sebastian. *Of Time, Work, and Leisure.* New York: Twentieth Century Fund, 1962.

Harris, Ann Sutherland. "The Second Sex in Academe," *AAUP Bulletin*, 56 (September 1970), pp. 283–95.

Hedges, Janice N. "Women Workers and Manpower Demands in the 1970's," *Monthly Labor Review*, 93 (June 1970), pp. 19–29.

Hiestand, Dale L. *Economic Growth and Employment Opportunities for Minorities.* New York: Columbia University Press, 1964.

Horner, Matina. "Women's Motive to Avoid Success," *Psychology Today*, 62 (November 1969), pp. 36–38.

Hunt, Morton M. *Her Infinite Variety.* New York: Harper and Row, 1962.

Hyatt, Jim. "Women at Work," *Wall Street Journal*, September 21, 1970.

Interdepartmental Committee on the Status of Women. *American Women, 1963–1968.* Washington: U.S. Government Printing Office, 1968.

Jones, Beverly, and Judith Brown. "Toward a Female Liberation Movement," *Voices from Women's Liberation*, ed. Leslie B. Tanner. New York: New American Library, 1970.

Kaplan, D. L., and Claire Casey. *Occupational Trends in the United States, 1900 to 1950.* U. S. Bureau of the Census, Working Paper No. 5, 1958.

Kerr, Clark. "The Balkanization of Labor Markets," *Labor Mobility and Economic Opportunity*, ed. E. Wight Bakke *et al.* New York: John Wiley and Sons, Inc., 1954.

Koerner, James. *Miseducation of American Teachers.* Boston: Houghton Mifflin, 1963.

Komarovsky, Mirra. *Blue Collar Marriage.* New York: Doubleday and Company, Inc., 1964.

Koontz, Elizabeth. "Not Just for Pin Money." U. S. Department of Labor, Women's Bureau, June 1970.

Koster, Marvin. "Income and Substitution Parameters in a Family Labor Supply Model." Unpublished Ph.D. dissertation, University of Chicago, 1966.

Kreps, Juanita M. "Sex and the Scholarly Girl," *AAUP Journal,* 51 (March 1965), pp. 30–33.

Kuh, Edwin. "Measurement of Potential Output," *American Economic Review,* 56 (September 1966), pp. 758–76.

Kyrk, Hazel. "Who Works and Why," *Annals of the American Academy of Political and Social Science,* 251 (May 1947), pp. 44–52.

Lavin, David E. *The Prediction of Academic Performance.* New York: Russell Sage Foundation, 1965.

Levinson, Perry. "How Employable are AFDC Women?" *Welfare in Review,* 8 (July–August 1970), pp. 12–16.

Lloyd-Jones, Esther. "Education for Reentry into the Labor Force," National Manpower Council, *Work in the Lives of Married Women.* New York: Columbia University Press, 1958.

Long, Clarence D. *The Labor Force Under Changing Income and Employment.* National Bureau of Economic Research. Princeton: Princeton University Press, 1958.

Lopate, Carole. *Women in Medicine.* Baltimore: Johns Hopkins Press, 1968.

Low, Seth, and Pearl G. Spindler. "Child Care Arrangements of Working Mothers in the United States." Children's Bureau Publication No. 461. Washington: U. S. Government Printing Office, 1968.

Lynd, Robert. *Knowledge for What: The Place of Social Sciences in American Culture.* New York: Grove Press, 1964.

Maccoby, Eleanor (ed.). *The Development of Sex Differences.* Stanford: Stanford University Press, 1966.

Mace, David, and Vera Mace. *The Soviet Family.* New York: Doubleday, Dolphin Books, 1964.

Mattfeld, Jacquelyn A., and Carol G. Van Aken (eds.). *Women and the Scientific Professions.* Cambridge: The M. I. T. Press, 1965.

Matthews, Esther. "The Marriage-Career Conflict in the Career Development of Girls and Young Women." Unpublished Ph.D. dissertation, Harvard University, 1960.

McClelland, David. *The Achieving Society.* New York: D. Van Nostrand, 1961.

Mead, Margaret, and Frances Balgley Kaplan (eds.). *American Women: Report of the President's Commission on the Status of Women.* New York: Charles Scribner's Sons, 1965.

Meade, E. M. "The Employment of Married Women," *The Three Bank Review,* No. 74. (June 1967).

Michel, Andree. "Needs and Aspirations of Married Women Workers in France," *International Labour Review,* 94 (July 1966), pp. 1–15.

Miller, Herman P. "Profile of the Blue-Collar American," Chapter 3 in *Blue Collar Worker,* ed. Sar Levitan. New York: McGraw-Hill, 1971.

Millet, Kate. *Sexual Politics.* New York: Doubleday and Company, 1970.

Mincer, Jacob. "Labor Force Participation of Married Women: A Study of Labor Supply," in National Bureau of Economic Research, *Aspects of Labor Economics.* Princeton: Princeton University Press, 1962.

Morgan, James N., et al. *Income and Welfare in the United States.* New York: McGraw-Hill, 1962.

————, Ismail Sirageldin, and Nancy Baerwaldt. *Productive Americans.* Monograph 43. Ann Arbor: University of Michigan Survey Research Center, 1966.

National Education Association. Research Bulletin, 44 (May 1966), pp. 50–57.

National Manpower Council. *Womanpower.* New York: Columbia University Press, 1957.

Oppenheimer, Valerie Kincade. *The Female Labor Force in the United States.* Population Monograph Series, No. 5. Berkeley: University of California, 1970.

Osofsky, Joy D. "The Socialization and Education of American Women," in Ann F. Scott, *What is Happening to American Women.* Atlanta: Southern Newspaper Publishing Association Foundation, 1970.

Packard, Vance. *The Sexual Wilderness: The Contemporary Upheaval in Male-Female Relationships.* New York: David McKay Co., 1968.

Parnes, Herbert S. *Research on Labor Mobility: An Appraisal of Research Findings in the United States.* New York: Social Science Research Council, 1954.

Parrish, John B. "Coming Crisis in Women's Higher Education and Work," *AAUW Journal,* 64 (November 1970), pp. 17–19.

————. "Professional Womanpower as a National Resource," *Quarterly Review of Education and Business* (1961), pp. 54–63.

————. "Soviet Womanpower as a Professional Resource," *Quarterly Review of Economics and Business*, 4 (Autumn 1964), pp. 55–61.

Parsons, Talcott. "Age and Sex in the Social Structure of the United States," *Essays in Sociological Theory*. Glencoe, Ill.: The Free Press, 1954.

Peters, David W. *The Status of the Married Woman Teacher*. New York: Bureau of Publications, Teachers College, Columbia University, 1934.

Petersen, Esther. "Working Women," *Daedalus*, 93 (Spring 1964), pp. 671–99.

Pigou, H. C. *The Economics of Welfare*. London: Macmillan, 1924.

"Profile of the Woman Engineer." New York: Society of Women Engineers, 1963.

Rainwater, Lee, *et al. Workingman's Wife*. New York: Oceana, 1959.

Ridley, Jeanne Clare. "Demographic Change and the Roles and Status of Women," *Annals of the American Academy of Political and Social Science*, 375 (January 1968), pp. 15–25.

Riley, Matilda W., Marilyn E. Johnson, and Sarane S. Boocock. "Woman's Changing Occupational Role—A Research Report," *American Behavioral Scientist*, 9 (May 1963), pp. 33–37.

Robinson, John. *The Workday*. Ann Arbor: Institute for Social Research, University of Michigan, 1967.

Rossi, Alice S. "Equality Between Sexes: An Immodest Proposal," *Daedalus*, 93 (Spring 1964), pp. 607–53.

————. "Women in Science: Why So Few?" *Science*, 148 (May 1965), pp. 1196–1202.

Schiffman, Jacob. "Marital and Family Characteristics of Workers," *Monthly Labor Review*, 84 (April 1961).

Shallcross, Ruth. *Should Married Women Work?* Public Affairs Pamphlet No. 49, 1940.

Shamseddine, Ahmad Hassein. *The Economics and Business Bulletin*. Philadelphia: Temple University, 1968.

Simon, Rita J., and Evelyn Rosenthal. "Profile of the Woman Ph.D. in Economics, History, and Sociology," *AAUW Journal*, 60 (March 1967), pp. 127–29.

Sirageldin, Ismail H. *Non-Market Components of National Income*. Ann Arbor: University of Michigan Survey Research Center, 1969.

Smuts, Robert W. "The Female Labor Force: A Case Study in the

Interpretation of Historical Statistics," *Journal of the American Statistical Association*, 55 (March 1960), pp. 71–79.

————. *Women and Work in America*. New York: Columbia University Press, 1959.

Spengler, Joseph J. "Product-Adding Versus Product-Replacing Innovations," *Kyklos*, 10 (Fasc. 3, 1957), pp. 267–77.

Stein, Robert L. "The Economic Status of Families Headed by Women," *Monthly Labor Review*, 93 (December 1970), pp. 3–10.

Steinmann, Anne. "The Ambivalent Woman," *New Generation*, 51 (Fall 1969), pp. 29–32.

Stirling, Betty. "The Interrelation of Changing Attitudes and Changing Conditions with Reference to the Labor Force Participation of Wives." Unpublished Ph.D. dissertation, University of California, 1963.

Terry, Geraldine B., and Alvin L. Bertrand. *The Labor Force Characteristics of Women in Low-Income Rural Areas of the South*. Southern Cooperative Series Bulletin 116, June 1966.

Turner, Marjorie B. *Women and Work*. Los Angeles: Institute of Industrial Relations, University of California, 1964.

United Nations Commission on the Status of Women. *Participation of Women in the Economic and Social Development of Their Countries*. New York: United Nations Publications, 1970.

U.S. Department of Labor, Bureau of Labor Statistics. *College Educated Workers, 1968–80*. Washington: U.S. Government Printing Office, 1970.

————. *Manpower Report of the President*, 1970.

————, Women's Bureau. *Changes in Women's Occupations 1940–50*. Bulletin No. 253. Washington: U.S. Government Printing Office, 1954.

————, Women's Bureau. *College Women Seven Years After Graduation*. Bulletin No. 292. Washington: U.S. Government Printing Office, 1966.

————, Women's Bureau. *Handbook of Women Workers, 1969*. Bulletin No. 294. Washington: U.S. Government Printing Office, 1970.

————, Women's Bureau. *Laws on Sex Discrimination in Employment*. Washington: U.S. Government Printing Office, 1970.

————, Women's Bureau. *Negro Women in the Population and in the Labor Force*. Washington: U.S. Government Printing Office, 1968.

————, Women's Bureau. *Sex Discrimination in Employment Practices*. Report on a conference held at University of California at

Los Angeles. Washington: U.S. Government Printing Office, 1970.

―――, Women's Bureau. *Trends in Educational Attainment of Women.* Washington: U.S. Government Printing Office, 1970.

―――, Women's Bureau. "Who are the Working Mothers?" Leaflet No. 37. Washington: U.S. Government Printing Office, 1970.

Waldman, Elizabeth. "Changes in the Labor Force Activity of Women," *Monthly Labor Review*, 93 (June 1970), pp. 10–18.

―――. "Marital and Family Characteristics of the U.S. Labor Force," *Monthly Labor Review*, May 1970, pp. 18–27.

Westervelt, Esther M. "Education, Vocation, and Avocation in Women's Lives," in Ann F. Scott, *What is Happening to American Women.* Atlanta: Southern Newspaper Publishing Association Foundation, 1970.

White, Martha S. "Psychological and Social Barriers to Women in Science," *Science*, 170 (October 1970), pp. 413–16.

Winick, Charles. *The New People: Desexualization in American Life.* New York: Pegasus, 1968.

Woody, Thomas. *A History of Women's Education in the United States*, Vol. I. New York: The Science Press, 1929.

Working Women in Large Cities. Fourth Annual Report of the U. S. Commissioner of Labor, 1888. Quoted in the *Monthly Labor Review*, 93 (June 1970).

Yudkin, Simon, and Anthea Holme. *Working Mothers and Their Children.* London: Michael Joseph and Co., 1963.

Zapoleon, Marguerite. "College Women and Employment," *The Education of Women: Signs for the Future*, ed. Opal D. David. Washington: American Council on Education, 1959.

Zazewski, Henry C. *Child Care Arrangements of Full-Time Working Mothers.* Children's Bureau Publication No. 378. Washington: U.S. Department of Health, Education and Welfare, 1959.

117